GITCHIE GIRL UNCOVERED

THE TRUE STORY OF A NIGHT OF MASS MURDER AND THE HUNT FOR THE DERANGED KILLERS

PHIL HAMMAN & SANDY HAMMAN

Authors of the best-selling true-crime memoir *Gitchie Girl*

first century principles.
a twenty-first century approach.

Gitchie Girl Uncovered: The True Story of a Night of Mass Murder and the Hunt for the Deranged Killers
By Phil Hamman & Sandy Hamman

Copyright 2019 by Phil Hamman & Sandy Hamman
Cover Design by eLectio Publishing

ISBN-13: 978-1-63213-700-5
Published by eLectio Publishing, LLC
Little Elm, Texas
http://www.eLectioPublishing.com

Printed in the United States of America

5 4 3 2 1 eLP 24 23 22 21 20 19

The eLectio Publishing editing team is comprised of: Christine LePorte, Lori Draft, Sheldon James, Court Dudek, and Jim Eccles.

Without limiting the rights under copyright reserved above, no part of this publication may be reproduced, stored in or introduced into a retrieval system, or transmitted, in any form, or by any means (electronic, mechanical, photocopying, recording, or otherwise), without the prior written permission of both the copyright owner and the above publisher of this book.

If you purchased this book without a cover, you should be aware that this book is stolen property. It was reported as "unsold and destroyed" to the publisher and neither the author nor the publisher has received any payment for the "stripped book."

The scanning, uploading, and distribution of this book via the Internet or via any other means without the permission of the publisher is illegal and punishable by law. Please purchase only authorized electronic editions, and do not participate in or encourage electronic piracy of copyrighted materials. Your support of the author's rights is appreciated.

Publisher's Note
The publisher does not have any control over and does not assume any responsibility for author or third-party websites or their content.

It is the duty of moral people
to bring justice to a world
where evil seeks to rule.

Phil Hamman

The definition of strength
is emerging from hard times
with a soft spirit.

Sandy Hamman

Dedicated to:

*The four boys and what they enjoyed in life:
Roger's love of the outdoors,
Stewart and Dana's dedication to music,
and Mike's passion for sports.*

*All law enforcement personnel
who protect our rights
and the freedoms we so cherish.*

*Sandra and her courage
in showing us how to move forward
no matter what life puts in our paths.*

Contents

Acknowledgments ix
A Note to the Readers xi
Chapter 1 1
Chapter 2 7
Chapter 3 13
Chapter 4 21
Chapter 5 31
Chapter 6 35
Chapter 7 41
Chapter 8 43
Chapter 9 45
Chapter 10 49
Chapter 11 57
Chapter 12 59
Chapter 13 61
Chapter 14 65
Chapter 15 67
Chapter 16 71

Chapter 17	75
Chapter 18	81
Chapter 19	85
Chapter 20	91
Chapter 21	99
Chapter 22	107
Chapter 23	117
Chapter 24	127
Chapter 25	131
Chapter 26	135
Chapter 27	137
Chapter 28	143
Chapter 29	147
Chapter 30	151
Chapter 31	161
Chapter 32	165
Chapter 33	181
Chapter 34	185
Chapter 35	187
Chapter 36	195
A Special Note from Sandra Cheskey	199
Other Credits	201
About the Authors	205

Acknowledgments

GRATITUDE DOESN'T BEGIN to express our appreciation to eLectio Publishing.

Thank you to Angela Houser and Amy Schmidt for your meticulous work in editing this book.

We could not have told this story so completely without the countless hours of input through personal interviews, emails, and phone calls with former Iowa BCI agents Lynn Ford, Terry Johnson, Bob Pontius, J.D. Smith, and Allen Steinbeck and former Lyon County Deputy Leroy Griesse. Your dedication to detail was exemplary. We greatly appreciate the personal stories shared by the children of Sheriff Craig Vinson: Tom Vinson, Janey Pullen, and Peggy Underberg. Thank you to the employees of the Dickinson and Lyon County Clerk of Courts offices who helped us access public information regarding the crimes. We are grateful to all who shared their personal experiences related to the Gitchie Manitou murders. Your stories touch our hearts and brought us closer to these tragic events. We appreciate the willingness of Bill Hadrath and Lynette Hadrath Dahl for relating their family's personal story regarding the loss of their brother at Gitchie

Manitou. A special thanks to Connie Nelson, Marissa Wollmann, and Marcia Gnadt, who arranged for us to visit the farms where Sandra was taken by the killers when she was kidnapped. Special thanks to Sylvia Fluit, who meticulously kept countless newspaper clippings from around the region related to the Gitchie crimes and to her daughter Sandy Bakker, who gave us access to all the articles.

Above all, bless you, Sandra, for bravely sharing your personal story of heartache and triumph in order to inspire all who read this.

A Note to the Readers

WHEN WE WROTE *Gitchie Girl: The Survivor's Inside Story of the Mass Murders that Shocked the Heartland*, the primary theme was to share Sandra Cheskey's struggles following the Gitchie Manitou mass murders. The book was her story. There were so many untruths and even vicious rumors circulating about that fateful night. We felt compelled to share who Roger Essem, Mike Hadrath, Stewart Baade, and Dana Baade were as good-natured teenagers with hopes, interests, and goals in life. So many people only knew them as murder victims. Along with this, there was much mystery and controversy surrounding the lone survivor, Sandra, that needed to be clarified. Sandra was silent about that night for over forty years. Why? In 1973, society held little compassion for a rape victim. Not everyone, of course, but so many felt that she deserved what she got. She shouldn't have been at Gitchie. What was she wearing that provoked the rape? Why was she out at night with a group of boys? Blaming the victim confirm that I'm not like her or I'm smarter, and this would never happen to me. It helps people distance themselves from ugly realities.

But what a difficult time for Sandra, who was only thirteen years old. She kept it all inside and conditioned herself to not talk or think about Gitchie Manitou. She distanced herself from society. She falsely convinced herself she had moved on, but the reality was that the horrors of the crime were gnawing away at her emotional well-being year after year and even resulted in physical health problems. Then she read Phil Hamman's memoir, *Under the Influence*, about growing up surrounded by domestic violence and poverty but somehow still overcoming the odds. Sandra was filled with the idea that maybe she too should speak out so that her story could help others. She had no idea that telling her story would help her as well. When we had our first book signings at Zandbroz and Barnes & Noble in Sioux Falls, hundreds of people showed up. The support Sandra received changed the way she started viewing herself, and this we attribute to the readers who give her the love and support for which she yearned. You helped to change her life. You made a difference.

As *Gitchie Girl* grew in popularity, people began craving more information, which gave life to the idea of a second book. There are still the strange twists, the bizarre coincidences, the unheralded investigative team that chased down the killers, and more about the three murderous brothers. In our first book, we refer to one of the brothers as J.R. He also went by the nickname "Sneaky," which we use in this book. In *Gitchie Girl Uncovered*, we fill in so many of these missing pieces. We spent a day with several of the BCI agents, and their memories of the investigation were so vivid it was as if we had gone back in time to 1973 and were there with them.

The conversations in this book come from investigative records and interviews, court transcripts, and occasionally the recollections of the people involved. Thank you to our readers for all of the support and feedback we have received.

—Phil & Sandy Hamman

Chapter 1

February 13, 2016
Barnes & Noble Bookstore, Sioux Falls, SD

SANDRA CHESKEY HAD BEEN trapped in a cocoon of emotional pain for decades. Now, unknown to everyone, including Sandra herself, the beautiful butterfly was about to emerge. Wearing a brightly colored tropical dress, her hair pulled into a wispy bun, she sat off to the side of an elevated coffee bar among spacious rows of books. A line of people, over one hundred with more entering behind them, weaved through the store to get a glimpse of the elusive "Gitchie Girl" and have a chance to talk with her. But Sandra, soft-spoken and uncomfortable in the spotlight, wasn't prepared to speak to the unexpected crowd with books in hand waiting for her autograph.

"I've thought about you so many times over the years and wondered how you were doing," one lady said with such sincerity that Sandra's eyes welled up.

Throughout the book signing several women leaned in and whispered in her ear, "I was sexually assaulted, too. You're my hero."

"For all these years, I thought no one cared," Sandra said to the group. "But look at *all* of these people!"

Hours later after the line had thinned, Sandra finally stood and spoke to those still crowded around her and eager to hear her story. She spoke deliberately. "When the trials were going on, one of the attorneys tried to protect me by telling me to walk with my head down so that the media couldn't get a picture of my face. For over forty years, I've been walking with my head down." She swallowed hard and shook her head. "After today, after all of your kind wishes, your caring words, your support, and being able to share my story, I'm finally healing. Now I can start walking with my head *up. Thank you!*"

"You are an inspiration, Sandra!" someone responded.

After forty-two years, the butterfly emerged. The tough little girl from Gitchie was back.

* * *

November 17, 1973
Gitchie Manitou State Park

BY NOVEMBER, THE BRIGHT hues have drained from the Midwest wildflowers and prairie grasses; leaves have formed dull brown blankets around barren trees in fields void of color. But with the temperatures being mild, Gitchie Manitou State Park retained its lure and beckoned a group of five friends as it had with so many other teenagers over many weekends, over many years. The park crosses the Iowa border a few miles east of Sioux Falls, South Dakota. It is a popular spot for hiking, camping, or fishing along the Big Sioux River, and the vanload of teens planned to build a fire and enjoy a late-fall evening among the brambly bushes beside a lazy river.

Despite its dents and streaks of rust, eighteen-year-old Stewart "Stew" Baade took quiet pride in his 1967 blue Chevy van that was rattling along a tar road headed east outside of Sioux Falls. The high school senior worked long hours at UPS outside of school to earn enough money to buy his own vehicle which, due to his generous nature, he often used to cart his friends around as he did on this mild night. With him were his fourteen-year-old brother, Dana, and three other friends, seventeen-year-old Roger Essem, fifteen-year-old Mike Hadrath, and thirteen-year-old Sandra Cheskey. When Deep Purple's "Smoke on the Water" started pounding from the radio, they sang along with the lyrics, and even Dana, who was usually quiet, played his air guitar with the same enthusiasm reserved for private lessons from his older brother, now at the wheel. The tune fit the mood of this 1973 evening, a time when Vietnam and the counterculture dominated the sentiment of many teens. Stew and the boys were on par with the times and as aspiring musicians scraped together enough extra cash to buy a marijuana joint, though they drove around for nearly two hours in search of someone who would sell such a small amount of weed.

Autumn's glowing pink and red sunset dissolved into a moonless black night accompanied by an ill-boding fog that thickened with the dropping temperatures and settled among the leafless trees of Gitchie Manitou, an area still spattered with ancient Native American burial mounds. The van's headlights illuminated just enough of the surroundings for the teenagers to get their bearings inside the park. They burst out of the van and strolled through the dark, untroubled by the thick fog settling around them and unaware of the horrors awaiting just down the path.

"Get some paper from the van for kindling," Stew directed Dana while the rest of the group gathered some wood which Roger and Dana soon turned into a roaring fire, a glowing pocket of fiery orange in the heavy darkness. The friends sat on fallen logs, laughing about the week's events, until unexpected crunching and snapping beyond the darkened tree line stifled the jubilation.

"Be quiet for a minute," Mike said with the confidence of a leader generated by years of being his basketball team's point guard and taking charge as the baseball team's pitcher, "I hear something."

The others nodded; they heard it too, but when they fell silent, the strange sounds faded. They were unnatural sounds that spooked them.

"It's just a wild animal," Roger said, perhaps to comfort his girlfriend, Sandra. Since meeting last summer, the two had gone on a few group dates, and he was the one who arranged this leisurely evening.

None of them had an inkling that evil had entered the park that murky night. Three deviant men nicknamed "The Boss," "Hatchet Face," and "Sneaky" had arrived, their shotguns loaded with .00 buckshot. Each shell contained high-velocity gunpowder and large, lethal BBs. One buckshot round would be the equivalent of being shot multiple times with a rifle projectile. After spying on the teenagers, Hatchet Face snuck back through the woods and underbrush to report what he saw around the campfire.

Several minutes later, Roger went to gather more wood and stood in the spot where the edges of flickering light faded into darkness, when suddenly three figures emerged on a rock ledge ten yards from the campfire. A terrifying explosion echoed through the park. Deadly pellets struck Roger's face and throat, and the force slammed him to the ground, where his suddenly lifeless body lay spread-eagle on the cold grass. Shouts erupted and another shot hit Stew. Sandra froze at the sound of gunfire, and Dana scrambled for cover. Mike grabbed Sandra by the arm and pulled her along until they reached the safety of a large tree.

"What's going on?" Sandra whispered to Mike after seeking refuge from the booming sound of the shotguns. Mike responded, "I don't know." They peered into the clearing where just moments before they were an innocent band of kids enjoying a night together. After a moment of silence, Mike and Sandra heard Stew cry out in agony, "I'm hit! They shot me!"

Sandra clung to Mike, and they cringed in unison at Stew's shouts. Everything went eerily still. Sandra's heart raced, and she gasped for breath. Then the quiet campsite was again broken by agonizing moans, and Stew's pain-wracked voice wailed, "Oh, God help me! It hurts so bad!" Sandra shivered, nearly paralyzed with fear. Even though it was dark, she shifted to see Mike's response and took some comfort in finding that his shadowy face remained stoic.

"Stay still. Be quiet," Mike whispered to Sandra. They could see the silhouettes of the three assailants shuffling about the dim firelight and saying something muffled to each other. Sandra trembled, reached out for Mike's arm, and was contemplating what they should do next when a deep voice sliced through the silence.

"We're the police, and this is a raid! Come out with your hands up!"

Wondering what to do, Sandra looked to Mike. His face was filled with disappointment, perhaps because he was the standout athlete who'd never once been in trouble with the law and was well-respected by peers and teachers alike. Mike moved from behind the tree and slowly raised his arms into the air. Sandra did the same. She saw Dana approaching from his hiding spot.

"What did we do?" Mike asked.

Before sunrise, the four boys lay dead on the ground. But by a miracle, Sandra was still alive. The three killers had "plans" for the innocent girl that included abducting and sexually assaulting her. By morning light, the three assailants went their separate ways.

CHAPTER 2

**Flashback to Sandra's beginning
September 1, 1960
Outside of Gettysburg, SD**

LOLO CHESKEY FINISHED a long shift at work and went to retrieve her three young boys from their babysitter. She'd almost reached the front door when a stabbing cramp gripped her stomach. Just down the road of this small farming community, eighteen-year-old Joyce was sitting down to a meal of pork chops and mashed potatoes with her mother, Barbara, when their evening was interrupted by the ringing telephone. The night was about to take an unusual turn. Joyce considered herself a typical girl who helped care for the numerous animals on her parents' farm, even assisting her father with the delivery of calves and piglets. She learned from a young age to work hard, so even in rare moments of free time, she busied herself by pulling out the bowls and measuring cups to whip up a dessert for the family supper. Her specialty was green apple pie. Others viewed her as humbly altruistic, a trait she likely inherited from her mother, Barbara, the town's third-grade teacher and a person known for her willingness to help others, even strangers. The two women shared a close relationship, and Joyce considered her mom to be the kindest person she'd ever met. Joyce's compassion led her to a job as a nurse's aide at the local Gettysburg Memorial Hospital in rural South Dakota. It was a small hospital with only a few beds, which resulted in Joyce becoming knowledgeable in an array of nursing services that were about to come in handy. When Barbara put down her fork to answer the ringing phone, she was taken aback by the urgent tone of her nearest neighbor.

"Lolo just got here and has gone into labor!" the babysitter said in a rush. Barbara had never met Lolo, so the neighbor explained who this lady was and how her contractions began, but she didn't know anyone who could take Lolo to the hospital.

"I'll watch her boys if you can give her a ride," the babysitter added.

The fact that Barbara had never met Lolo didn't stop her from agreeing to help.

"Come with me, Joyce," Barbara insisted, knowing it was only a ten-minute drive to the Gettysburg hospital yet thinking it wise to have an additional person in the car just in case.

The mother-daughter team quickly helped Lolo into the car and took off for the hospital, but when they arrived, Lolo gritted her teeth and with a look of concern explained, "Not this hospital! I need to go to the Eagle Butte Indian Hospital."

"Lolo! That's seventy-five miles away. We're right here at Memorial."

"No, no. I have long labors. I need to go to Eagle Butte where I won't have to pay for the delivery."

"I don't know, Lolo…"

"All of my labors have been the same. They're long, and the contractions just started. We have enough time. I don't have the money to pay the hospital here."

Being part Native American, Lolo was enrolled as a member of the Cheyenne River Sioux Indian tribe. In accordance with federal laws, members are allotted free medical treatment but only at certain native-based facilities. Lolo's marriage hung by a thread. Her husband was in the service and was not sending any money home, and Lolo's job didn't quite cover the expenses she managed on her own. Doing whatever she had to in order to make ends meet had become second nature.

Barbara reluctantly agreed, shifted the car into drive, and headed west on an unfamiliar road to Eagle Butte. It was nearly sundown, and they found themselves driving right into the setting sun. In spite of this, Barbara drove as quickly as she safely could on what proved to be a challenging and tense journey. The blinding glint of sun slowly disappeared, leaving them in total blackness on the weather-beaten tar road that was not only winding but peppered with nocturnal creatures scampering across their path. Joyce gasped when Barbara slammed on the brakes to avoid hitting two whitetail deer that had bolted just inches in front of the headlights. The jarring motion only drew a small groan from Lolo, who was quietly bearing intense labor pains. Barbara gripped the wheel and leaned forward to concentrate on the dangerous curves. At times, raccoons, skunks, and more deer caused the pace of the drive to slow to a crawl while the labor pains raced with each contraction. Lolo barely grimaced or even made a sound. As a veteran teacher, Barbara became accustomed to noticing small changes not only in her students but in others as well. A creased brow might indicate a confused child who was too embarrassed to raise his hand, while a row of jittery children meant it was time for recess. About twenty miles from Eagle Butte, she heard Lolo's breathing grow rapid, and it became apparent that the baby would be arriving before they could reach the hospital.

Barbara pulled over to the side of the road. "That baby is coming now!" she said and tossed her daughter, Joyce, a towel. Lolo lay down in the back seat and prepared herself for the arrival of this baby. Even under the dim dome light, it was clear that the baby's head was already crowning. With a maturity beyond her years, Joyce guided Lolo through the brief delivery. The baby arrived, and the car was filled with a tense quiet. Joyce wiped the tiny newborn's face, cleared the fluids from the baby's silent mouth, and began stimulating the child's back. A heavy and worried silence settled inside the car, and Joyce could hear nothing but her own labored breathing. When the first lusty cry finally burst forth, Barbara shouted from the front seat, "Thank God!"

Once the placenta was delivered, Joyce wrapped it and the little girl in the towel and handed the bundle to Lolo, who began nursing the still screaming baby. Barbara pulled back onto the road and continued driving while Joyce massaged Lolo's uterus as the nurses taught her to do when helping newly delivered mothers at the hospital. While pressing down firmly, she noticed the baby stopped crying, so she glanced up only to find the newborn suckling vigorously. This indication of a healthy baby gave Joyce a measure of relief.

When they arrived at Indian Health Services over thirty minutes later, the medical facility was dark. Joyce sprinted up the steps and rang the doorbell repeatedly until a night nurse showed up. Joyce walked briskly alongside the nurse, explaining what transpired on the trip there. At this late hour, the only noise was the background humming of medical machines. The two raced down a hall where the nurse grabbed a wheelchair, which she used to bring Lolo and the baby into the maternity wing. Joyce and Barbara watched them disappear into a set of double doors and looked at each other in disbelief at what they just experienced. Before they could leave, Joyce filled out a lengthy report describing the details of the birth.

"Is the baby in the nursery yet? Can we see her?" Barbara asked.

The nurse excused herself to check on the new patients and returned quickly. "The baby may be contaminated due to being born in a car, so she won't be going to the nursery. She's with her mother now," she explained as kindly as possible.

Joyce and Barbara then headed back to Gettysburg and arrived home emotionally and physically drained. They were too tired to clean the backseat, which was covered with dried blood and afterbirth, so they removed it from the car and leaned it against the side of the house, intending to wash it after getting some sleep. Joyce's father came in from doing chores late that night and had no idea what had transpired. He just went to bed. A loud pounding on the front door woke him the next morning; he was puzzled to find the sheriff standing there with a stern look on his face. A nosy neighbor had seen the bloody car seat and called the sheriff, assuming that homicide was the likeliest explanation for the gory scene.

"I'm investigating a call regarding a murder that took place," the sheriff said to Joyce's dad, who had no idea what he was talking about so went and woke up his wife and daughter, who were just as surprised to find the law at their door. The sheriff listened to their story, but his suspicions were not easily allayed, so he checked it all out with the Eagle Butte Hospital, which put the matter to rest. Years later, Joyce reminisced that the birth of Sandra Cheskey *was actually a very noncomplicated delivery, except, of course, one usually does not deliver in the backseat of a Chevy.* Sandra's future, however, would prove to be anything but noncomplicated.

CHAPTER 3

November 18, 1973
Gitchie Manitou State Park

A COUPLE TEST-DRIVING a new car on the morning of November 18th decided to loop through Gitchie Manitou State Park where they soon came upon three figures lying in the matted-down grass. Thinking it was kids playing a prank, the man shook his head and beeped his horn. When he stepped out of the car for a closer look, he saw smears of blood and drag marks in the dry, brown grass. He drove quickly back to the park's entrance, where he saw another car starting to pull in. The man rolled down his window. "There are dead bodies down the road! Don't go in. Could you block this entrance so no one else can go there?" He drove to the nearest farmhouse and called the authorities, who contacted police officers from Sioux Falls as well as Lyon County Sheriff Craig Vinson and his one deputy, Leroy Griesse, who began scrambling to get organized for a high-profile investigation.

By early afternoon, Bureau of Criminal Investigation agent Terry Johnson received the call to assist Sheriff Vinson's office with a mass murder. Johnson was responsible for six counties in northwest Iowa, and Lyon County was one of them. The Iowa BCI's purpose was to support local law enforcement agencies by providing investigative expertise, crime laboratory evidence collection and analysis, additional investigation personnel, and other services. Vinson and Griesse would still be responsible for the enormous daily responsibilities of running a jail and handling requests for law enforcement assistance in the county. They simply didn't have the manpower to conduct a major murder investigation in addition to the other duties.

Johnson had worked with Sheriff Vinson for several years. Prior to becoming a BCI agent, Johnson's interest in law enforcement began when as a child he would wear his uncle's FBI badge around the house. Years later, a job at the Morton Frozen Pie Plant turned out to be his tipping point. He spent the summer setting the scale so a machine would drop the right amount of crumbs into pie tins, a monotonous task which allowed him time to contemplate other careers. With his uncle's encouragement, Johnson passed the test to become a Webster City, Iowa police officer and rode a three-wheel Harley as a "cycle cop." The grind of writing speeding tickets and escorting funerals or parades had him itching for his near obsession with investigation. Now, six years after spotting a job opening with the BCI, Johnson was on the road to the biggest investigation of his entire law enforcement career, a mass murder in northwest Iowa.

He followed protocol and called Deputy Director Warren Stump at BCI headquarters in Des Moines to let him know about this assignment and to request that a crime lab crew and additional agents be sent to Lyon County as well. Stump was a goal-setting lawman who handled his high-pressure job in a fearless manner. Stump did, however, have one fear and that was flying, a form of transportation he tried to avoid. Standard procedure was for headquarters to assign other agents since the discovery of this many bodies constituted a major investigation which flooded the homicide department.

Time is of utmost importance in a homicide investigation, where leads can turn cold overnight. Johnson quickly relayed the limited information he had to Stump, packed a bag, and headed northwest to Rock Rapids, Iowa. While Johnson was on the road, police officers discovered that the boys were from Sioux Falls, South Dakota, which meant that their efforts would need to be coordinated with the local offices in another state. At headquarters, Stump assigned a team of reliable agents to work alongside Johnson, Sheriff Vinson, Deputy Griesse, and the team from Sioux Falls.

One BCI agent was Lynn Ford from Council Bluffs, Iowa, an intense twenty-eight-year-old Vietnam vet from the 2nd battalion, 9th Marines. After the war he needed a career and made his entrance into law enforcement as a state trooper for several years, but he was a newbie to the BCI, which earned him the designation of being a "boot." It was evening by the time he got the call to assist Johnson and thereby dark when he hopped into his state-issued green 1971 Plymouth for a cold drive straight north on icy roads.

Next was Allen "Al" Steinbeck, twenty-nine, whose interest in law enforcement developed its roots when he was a child growing up on a farm in Primgar, Iowa, where his family raised corn, beans, and livestock. He joined the US Navy when he was seventeen, right out of high school. After a three-year stretch in the Navy, he worked various jobs in San Diego and Iowa before applying to become an Iowa State Trooper. Like Ford, he eventually transferred from the patrol to the BCI.

Agent Bob Pontius was also assigned. He started out as a police officer in Yankton, South Dakota, before joining the ranks of the Iowa BCI. He picked up Steinbeck in Missouri Valley, Iowa, and they headed north nearly 180 miles to Gitchie Manitou.

Rounding out the BCI team was J.D. Smith, who grew up in Iowa's largest city, Des Moines, but moved to the quiet town of Red Oak in the western part of the state. J.D. was known to be headstrong and outspoken with an enviably quick wit that kept those around him on their toes. He used well-aimed wisecracks to needle obstructive co-workers when necessary and sometimes just for fun.

Each BCI agent was married but also had to be intensely committed to a job that pulled him away physically and emotionally for days or weeks on end. The Gitchie investigation proved to be the most intense case any of them would ever experience, filled with mounting pressure and sleepless nights.

Gitchie Manitou State Park is located in the extreme northwest corner of Iowa, where corn is king. It is surrounded in summer by abundant fields of towering green stalks that had now been harvested into brown stubble waiting for the first cover of winter snow. It is flanked by the states of South Dakota and Minnesota, which, along with Iowa, host acres of flat seed fields that stretch for great distances. The park has remained unchanged and is an oasis of unspoiled beauty amid the modern farms with towering silos and John Deere combines. Here, the winding Big Sioux River has carved steep banks among rolling hills sprinkled with pink outcropping rocks and ledges. Giant white oak, silver maple, and ash trees cast welcome shade on the tall grasses and native prairie flowers that fill the park. For thousands of years, Native Americans were drawn to this place of solitude where they honored their dead. The park still bears witness to numerous burial mounds that rise curiously from the otherwise gentle prairie.

By the time Johnson pulled into Gitchie Manitou a few hours later, deputies from Minnehaha County in South Dakota and Sioux Falls police detectives had already begun an investigation in the now somber park. He turned off the ignition and allowed himself a few moments to scan the surroundings and let his body flood with the focus of a seasoned agent. Dark settled in, along with another round of creeping fog, and the November chill only exacerbated the depressing atmosphere of the park. A gust of wind surged down the path to where he stood, kicking up bits of leaf. He walked to where floodlights, hooked up to portable generators, washed out the color around the crime scene and three bodies lay lifeless and riddled with gaping gunshot wounds. Their eyes were still open and staring as if pleading for justice. It was not a sight for the faint of heart and was an image difficult to shake when the investigators closed their own eyes at the end of many stressful days.

Each new arrival was greeted by Sheriff Vinson and apprised of the situation.

"There is a thirteen-year-old girl who survived the murders," Vinson informed Johnson, who was stunned by this news. "She gave a statement to Don Skadsen from the SFPD and myself. Her name is Sandra, and for her protection she's being temporarily housed at the Juvenile Detention Center."

It was decided that everyone would wait until the BCI crime lab arrived before approaching the bodies. Johnson's initial thought was that it was obvious they were killed with shotguns due to the devastating wounds and the large amounts of blood. Drag marks indicated they were pulled to this area but not from far away. Likely, he reasoned aloud, no one could dispose of the bodies quickly so they attempted to make them less visible. Theories came in waves. Did the boys come out with someone they knew? Had they been set up? Was dope involved? And in the midst of this, *Why me, Lord?* As quickly as the thought came, Johnson realized that the boys had probably thought the same thing sometime throughout their horrendous ordeal.

By the time Steinbeck and Pontius arrived, an ambulance was waiting with the engine running. The floodlights cast a dull white halo over the death scene. Tree branches blowing in the wind sent flickering shadows rippling across the three uncovered bodies. Steinbeck had responded to numerous accidents and deaths as a trooper, so while the scene didn't shock him, the sight of the young teenagers unsettled his core. He joined a group of officers standing about forty feet from the crime scene, waiting for the lab to arrive.

From farther down the path, a distant shout rang out. "We have another one over here!" A policeman discovered a fourth body closer to the river. Only Vinson and Johnson approached the victim but stood back far enough to not contaminate the site. From several feet away, agents took notes and despite the plummeting temperature, began discussing theories to give the investigation its first breaths of life. Long shadows spread across the park, enveloping it in black. In November, dark comes early in Iowa, so they held their positions rather than searching for clues. There was nothing else they could do until morning light. Before winding up for the night, Johnson thought to himself, *Why were they all here at once, and how did things get so bad?*

It now fell on Sheriff Vinson's shoulders to visit with each of the boys' families, tell them the bad news, and find out why the boys were at the park that night. Was it possible that someone forced the teenagers out to Gitchie? Were they aware of any motive for the crime? Unfortunately, none of the families had any information that could be developed into a lead. He collected a picture of each boy to release to the media and to use when bringing in potential suspects or witnesses.

CHAPTER 4

November 18, 1973
Rock Rapids, Iowa
Gitchie Manitou State Park

IT WAS A SCENE that haunted Cheri Henli for decades, the likes of which she'd never see again. With thick, brown hair that fell in waves to her shoulders, her outgoing demeanor fit her high energy level. After she married the drum major from college, the newlyweds moved to Rock Rapids in the northwest corner of Iowa where LeRoy Henli accepted a job as the middle school and elementary band teacher and Cheri the high school banner corps director. When the couple decided to join the town's volunteer ambulance squad, Cheri faced a towering obstacle; no woman had ever been part of the county's ambulance squad. It was considered a man's job and most doubted that a woman, especially one who weighed 107 pounds, had what it took to be an EMT. Cheri had to prove that she could lift a gurney the same as any man, a feat she was largely expected to fail. LeRoy believed in her but getting past the others proved difficult.

"How will she lift a two-hundred-fifty-pound man?" some of the EMTs questioned Alfred Goldman, a veteran member of the ambulance team who was significant enough to sway the will of skeptical residents. With his barrel chest and skinny legs, he was known more for his heart of gold than for his profession as a cattle inseminator; impregnating cows was a critical job in a small farming town. The gurneys at the time didn't have wheels and had to be lifted and carried by hand. Alfred and another prominent member of the ambulance team gave the other dozen or so members the okay to welcome her on board after she went on a few practice calls as a helper during her EMT training.

LeRoy took the midnight to 8 AM shift and Cheri 4 PM to midnight. That way either she or LeRoy would be available to stay with the kids. On the rare occasions when they were called at the same time, Cheri's mom came running without complaint as she did that night when, during the middle of dinner, their walkie-talkies went off. After answering the dispatcher, Cheri left the spaghetti on the table, pulled on warm clothing, and kissed her two young children goodnight.

Cheri squinted at her watch, trying to catch a glimpse of the time in the shimmer of headlights from an oncoming vehicle. Though only 6 PM, night came early in mid-November, and the ambulance hummed along back roads void of roadway lighting. The volunteer ambulance squad's goal was to be on the road in three to four minutes, and they beat it.

"Where are we going?" she called to Alfred from her jump seat in the back. It was her habit to picture the upcoming emergency call and prepare for what they might encounter by making a dry run of the scene in her head. This forethought allowed her time to organize supplies she might need, knowing that seconds could mean the difference between life and death.

The dispatcher won't tell us anything," Alfred said, seeming to ponder the confusion behind this secrecy. "They just said to go to Gitchie Manitou Park."

The headlights revealed fields of brown stubble whizzing by in brief flickers. Alfred knew the country roads better than anyone and raced at top speed. On sharp corners, Cheri had to grab onto something for support.

"Yep. It's pretty unusual," Alfred said without anyone prodding him. "I don't think I've ever *not* been told what kind of call I'm going on." He seemed edgy.

His words didn't sit well with Cheri. In this small community, Alfred was known for withholding his opinions and waiting until he had something important to say. It was due to his fair-handed objectivity that she was accepted by the others on the squad.

"You getting any heat back there?" Alfred asked, switching the topic.

Before long, he was pulling off the highway onto a pitch-black road that led to the entrance of Gitchie Manitou. A flashlight off to the side of the road flickered to life, and an arc of light directed them to stop just outside a temporary snow fence that was stretched across the entrance to the park. This roadblock took Cheri by surprise. The ambulance eased to a stop, and Alfred rolled down the window, straining into the blackness to see who was holding the flashlight when the shadowy figure of Deputy Griesse stepped into view. Griesse was known for his easy, outgoing manner; he was a cohesive force who was always ready with a joke or a laugh, but tonight he looked deflated. Cheri couldn't recall him ever looking this somber, which did nothing to ease the knot that had been squeezing her stomach.

"What happened out here?" Alfred asked after everyone gave their obligatory nods of recognition.

Griesse shook his head, looking as though he wished he didn't have to answer. "We have four young boys who've been shot." He paused in response to the gasps and murmurs from inside the ambulance. Alfred's eyebrows scrunched at the gravity of Griesse's voice. "There's a BCI Econoline van just down the road. You'll wait up there until the detectives finish up."

The local law enforcement expected the Econoline van to contain a state-of –the-art crime lab on wheels and were somewhat disheartened to discover it was stocked with little more than cameras and a few cardboard boxes onto which someone scrawled labels such as "Lab vials" and "Gloves."

"Shot? What happened?" Alfred asked.

"We can't confirm any more than that right now." Griesse glanced into the park then spoke through the ambulance window in a hushed whisper. "Honestly, I've been here at the entrance and don't know much more. It looks like a homicide though."

The word "homicide" hardly registered with any of them. Homicides happened somewhere else; not quiet Rock Rapids where many people did not even once in their lives lock their front doors. At the end of the road was the Econoline. Someone brought them steaming cups of coffee, and as they sipped, conversation about what might have transpired at the park filled the air.

"Who would have done this? Could it be someone we know?"

"Are the killers still out there?"

"Could be. It's only eight PM, and sometimes they return to the scene of the crime."

They all tried to figure out how four boys ended up getting shot.

"It could be someone who escaped from jail or prison. I imagine the detectives will check that out." Cheri scooted over to a window and peered out. The portable floodlights outside only cast a smear of white against the billowing fog, giving the park the appearance of an old black-and-white horror movie.

"I can't see anything," she reported, adding to the cheerless conversation that was little more than a guessing game. The time crawled from one hour to the next. By 1 AM, Cheri bit at the edge of her lip to keep from nodding off; the strong coffee had lost its edge. LeRoy needed to leave for work by seven that morning; though exhausted, he wouldn't consider sleeping on the job. None of them did.

Cheri rubbed at her doughy eyelids when at 4 AM, the door handle turned, and along with a rush of cold air, a BCI agent appeared. Just beyond him, more detectives placed boxes into a car under a fuzzy halo of light, and the distant noise of several detectives loading up to leave filtered through the open trailer door.

The agent introduced himself and repeated what Griesse told them hours ago. "You'll need to bring the bodies to Rock Rapids," he instructed and with the tilt of his head, pointed them in the direction of the police officer who would guide them to the bodies. Rock Rapids, they knew, meant the funeral home, as the funeral director was also the coroner. He would provide invaluable evidence as to what transpired the night of the murders, and it was the job of the ambulance drivers to deliver the boys there.

Anticipation morphed into anxiety outside the security of the van. Cheri hesitated but then led the way, and the three of them assembled around a police officer who flicked on a lone flashlight. The floodlights were now dismantled and the detectives gone, leaving them in a small circle of dull light that faded into blackness. The last of the cars rumbled down the road, and as the headlights disappeared, the park fell into black silence. A gust of cold wind sent shivers through her body, matching the feelings inside of her. It made Cheri realize that the sheer number of people had lent an air of security that now left a dreadful void into which she must walk. At once, her confidence drained away into the brittle air, leaving her consumed with the terrifying thought that the killers could be waiting only steps away. They walked in a pack, crunching leaves beneath their feet and following the thread of light that illuminated uneven ground. The waist-high grasses offered convenient hiding places. It took two minutes to reach the site but seemed longer. That's when Cheri saw the unspoken fear in Alfred's eyes. *Are the killers out there watching us?*

The policeman swung the flashlight at an angle to reveal three shapes on the ground, and all the ambulance personnel let out a moan of disbelief. A band of fog hung low, like a shroud draped over the bodies. The victims looked young. Cheri couldn't help but think that they were dressed like kids. They had kids' clothes on like they had just come from school.

"It looks like they were on their knees and then shot," one of the men lamented, noting that their hands were above their heads.

"Like an assassination," someone said. Gaping wounds riddled their young bodies.

"But they're just kids," Cheri gasped. A dark fear weaved its way into her subconscious, and she fought back the overwhelming thought of how terrified the boys must have felt before they fell. She prepared herself for the worst before every call. When called to a highway accident, she imagined a scene where there might be body parts to recover. Though gory, it was necessary to anticipate the worst in order to reduce the mental trauma and focus on the victims. Usually it wasn't as bad as she expected, but tonight was different. Nothing had prepared her for this emotional punch.

The shock hit too close for LeRoy, who worked with children this age. "I'm going to pass out," he admitted, and his knees weakened.

"Go sit down a minute," Cheri urged, grabbing him by the arm and leading him to a rock ledge.

She and Alfred hesitated briefly. Then Cheri knelt down, knowing she should emotionally remove herself from this job, but something kept pulling her mind to these young victims. Tears welled up thinking of her own children safe and warm in their beds at home. Then other images appeared. She saw these teenagers as little boys doing little boy things: running, catching frogs, and laughing. But Cheri didn't cry here. That would be for later. Then she felt compelled to do more. As though guided by an invisible force, she gave each boy a gentle rub on the arm, a mother's touch, as if they were her own children. Was it possible, she wondered, for a mysterious maternal thread to somehow let the boys' mothers know that even in death, loving hands were there? Her heart ached for the parents who that day received the news that every parent fears.

She and Alfred enclosed the first boy in a body bag, which seemed an act of warmth and protection, lifted him onto the stretcher, and walked along the path back to the ambulance in silence. They repeated the trip for the second boy. *Is the killer out there? Maybe he was watching us the first time, and now . . .* An overwhelming unease washed over her. She kept up with the police officer, who was swinging the flashlight back and forth, and with each sweep she expected the shadow of a gunman to appear.

Then suddenly the light caught LeRoy's shape standing and waiting for them, ready to go. It was his style, the same determination that found him marching with the band at 6 AM in rain or sleet without so much as a wisp of a thought to cancel practice. Cheri steeled herself for the trek to pick up the third boy, who was near the other two yet somehow looked out of place. His coat was bunched up and the body angle and positioning made it appear he was dragged there and dropped unceremoniously near the others.

"There are four boys, right?" Alfred asked, saying what Cheri wondered silently. They automatically looked around as if by some miracle one of them might spot a body through fog and dark.

"The last boy is down there." The officer motioned into the inky blackness with his flashlight but didn't say how far it was.

The walk down the trail was precarious. The flashlight's weak beam was inadequate, which caused the group to slip and stumble on loose rock and fallen branches. Cheri made mental notes to guide her way back since she'd be carrying a gurney that would block part of her vision.

It took less than eight minutes to reach the last boy, though it would have been much quicker in daylight. All the way down and back, Cheri had the haunting feeling that someone evil was out there in the dark. Her thighs burned, and she could hardly catch her breath by the time they reached the ambulance. The three worked together to attach the gurney to the hooks on the ceiling. There was room for two gurneys on the floor and two above. Even though the bodies were inside bags, she had an unnatural feeling that they might sit up or start speaking at any moment; it was a thought she'd never before experienced.

The road shook beneath her, which jostled the bodies, giving them the appearance of movement. Cheri gripped the window opening that separated her from the front seat, then trained her eyes on the four body bags, but only for a moment, wishing she could rekindle life into the still bodies through sheer willpower. Cheri felt their presence and couldn't look, couldn't face them. The trauma was too fresh and too personal. All at once she felt the combined impact of a lack of sleep and abundance of caffeine along with the traumatic scene at the park. When the ambulance started shimmying down the road, and the bodies bounced at each bump, she felt a strong urge to jump out. They traveled in near silence. With the boys right there, it seemed disrespectful to carry on a conversation as if nothing happened. Soon, Alfred pulled into the morgue, and somehow Cheri and LeRoy made their way home. It was 5 AM.

The ordeal was over, but both of them were overcome with sorrow. They hung up their winter coats, then stood in front of the closet still in heavy clothing and boots and held each other. LeRoy's comforting hands rubbed the small of her back that ached from the heavy lifting. In the morning silence, both of them stood stunned and trying to mentally process what they had just gone through. In the void of the living room, Cheri noticed the little things: a clock ticking, the refrigerator humming, and the furnace kicking on. The comforting home noises should have brought feelings of normality back, but they didn't. She was only partially aware of LeRoy eating a light breakfast, the first bite he had since dinner over twelve hours ago. He dressed without a word and left for school. Cheri's mom scrutinized her gravely, both fiercely proud and worried about the toll this volunteer job took on Cheri.

The blast of a shotgun tore past Cheri Henli's ear. She watched in horror as a crimson stain spread across the coat of the boy standing in front of her. He reached out to her with pleading arms, but she was too late. She screamed for someone to help, but the words caught in her throat and came out as a whisper. Her legs locked and turned to iron. She couldn't move, and if he fell it would be her fault. Someone was screaming in the distance, and she realized it was her own voice.

Cheri sat upright in bed as she did every time the same haunting dream reoccurred.

CHAPTER 5

November 19, 1973
Sioux Falls, SD & surrounding region

WHEN THE REGION woke up to front page headlines of the mass murder, shock and outrage swept through the community like an epidemic. At Sioux Falls Washington High, where Roger, Stew, and Mike attended school, and at Dana's Patrick Henry Junior High, the atmosphere turned dismal. Teachers whispered, and students stood in small clusters, some openly sobbing, and most largely unequipped to deal with the emotions that accompanied the senseless slaughter. Questions welled from local citizens who expected the crimes to be quickly solved, and the burden of answering these queries fell on the shoulders of the investigative team, which would grow to include multiple law enforcement agencies from the tri-state area. The job of solving the crime fell primarily on the Iowa Bureau of Criminal Investigation, a group whose purpose was to provide backup when requested by local agencies as Sheriff Vinson had immediately done. The BCI worked with the local offices rather than taking over, which made them comrades with a common goal rather than arrogant grandstanders.

In fact, the agents often became like family, a cohesive group of like-minded men.

Since the Lyon County Sheriff's Department still had their daily duties of patrolling, running the jail, and investigating local reports, they relied heavily on the Iowa BCI to investigate the Gitchie murders. Eventually, sixteen Iowa BCI agents, two South Dakota Department of Criminal Investigation agents, the Minnehaha and Lyon County Sheriff's departments, the Sioux Falls Police, South Dakota and Iowa State Patrol officers, and even the Department of Natural Resources joined forces with the expectation of solving this massive crime promptly. The question hung in the air as to how this many agencies would cooperate without stepping on toes or egos as is common with many investigations.

The gossip ran faster than the news reports could hit the streets. An anxious public craved more information but were only given bite-sized pieces to satisfy their hunger for this news. Weaving its way through this upheaval were murmurs that a young teenager survived the fateful night, and immediately anger and suspicion accompanied theories of why her life was spared. Fueling the skepticism and anger was the lack of any solid motive or leads on suspects.

The BCI agents had worked under the strong floodlights until nearly 3:00 on Monday, November 19, at which point the ambulance squad removed the bodies. The agents went back to their hotel, got a few hours of sleep, and returned to the park at daybreak. The hours immediately following a crime yield the "hottest" clues, and with each passing minute the proverbial trail begins to grow cold. It wasn't due to exhaustion that the agents left the scene the previous night, but rather that they'd done all they could under the limitations of the artificial light. They expected daylight to reveal new clues. The following day, they moved into the Holiday Inn in Sioux Falls, a gleaming ten-story building that boasted a rotating restaurant and was the new jewel of an otherwise aging downtown.

By the time the first glints of sun filtered through the leafless branches, all of the BCI investigators had already gathered at the park entrance. They moved toward the crime scene with attentiveness, their eyes trained to spot anything out of the ordinary amongst the underbrush garnished with rock ledges. Their discussions, edged with a serious tone, broke the silence at the otherwise silent park as they voiced their observations and scribbled notes while walking along the path. Then the cheerless talk fell suddenly silent at the campsite, where blackened timber and cold ashes bore witness to a night of terror. Off to the side, an acoustic guitar leaned against a tree as though it had been left there momentarily, its owner intending to return. This was ground zero, the dawn of both the crimes and the investigation, and it took mere minutes to divulge clues that were hidden by darkness the previous night.

"We have a blood trail," one of the agents said, motioning toward the ground.

Immediately, the others closed in on the vital evidence. The trail led away from the campsite in the direction where the three bodies were discovered. One of the men took photos, another took notes, and they all moved gradually along the path tracking the blood droplets that were visible not only on fallen leaves, grass, and rocks but splotched on the side of tree trunks and low-hanging branches. The blood, now dry and a deep crimson color, went along in a regular pattern for thirty yards. *Was someone wounded and attempting to escape?* Then appeared a clue of such significance the investigators were convinced it would help prove what happened that night. Before them was a large pool of blood and next to it an oval of matted grass nearly the size of a body.

CHAPTER 6

November 19, 1973
Sioux Falls Police Department

TERRY JOHNSON WAS the BCI agents' team leader and face of the investigation, delivering daily updates to the media with down-to-earth honesty to help quell the clamoring public. Due to the rarity of four teenagers being murdered, the tips were piling up, and he appointed J.D. Smith to assign these leads. The team was already stretched to its limit, straining to follow every tip while remaining diligent about not focusing on any one person right away lest a defense attorney jump on that in court by claiming *you targeted my client from the start and didn't look at anyone else.*

Besides furnishing manpower, the Sioux Falls Police provided the BCI with an unused wing of their building for the command center. Despite a slight dankness that settled into the unused wing, the accommodations were spacious and largely furnished with the equipment they needed. The BCI agents were given keys to the door leading to this wing, and it was locked whenever no one was present. Later in the investigation, a strange tip was found in this locked wing with suspicion as to how it arrived there.

Those who remained at Gitchie focused on the location of the fourth boy, Roger, who was found deeper in the woods close to the river and about one hundred yards from the other boys. A small section of the park was located in South Dakota while most of the park was located in Iowa. He was so close to the imaginary line that separated the two states that a surveyor was brought in to determine in which state Roger's body fell. If he was killed in South Dakota, then their state laws would take over and incur the cost of pursuing justice for Roger.

Meanwhile, Sheriff Vinson bristled with apprehension over his next task. On Monday, November 19th, he and Johnson met at the Sioux Falls police department to arrange for the lone survivor, Sandra, to walk them through the park and explain what transpired the other night. It seemed harsh to request this of Sandra, yet was vital to solving this case. The frail, soft-spoken thirteen-year-old with long, dark hair and chestnut eyes had completed a ten-page, handwritten witness statement the previous afternoon. On top of that she was fingerprinted, interrogated, and interviewed, and spent a sleepless night at the juvenile detention center where she was housed out of concern for her safety. She also endured a rape exam at the hospital, which proved she had been sexually assaulted. She was exhausted and sat with her head bowed, shoulders drooped, and arms crossed tightly across her waist. Through the thick door, muted conversations and the sound of footsteps on tile seeped in.

"Sandra, we need you to go back to the park and show us where the events of that night occurred. We need a videotaped statement from you at Gitchie Manitou," Vinson explained in a voice that conveyed both compassion and determination. The investigators were certain that the actual park might evoke even more facts that could be crucial. Her recollection of details the night of the murders was astonishing. She even claimed to remember that the tallest of the murderers, whom the others called The Boss, smoked Pall Mall cigarettes.

"How did he happen to tell you that he smoked Pall Malls?" Vinson asked. Either she was incredibly observant or perhaps more familiar with these murderers than anyone realized.

"Because I asked him," she replied quietly.

She even claimed that The Boss drove her home after she was raped but threatened to kill her if she went to the authorities. While Vinson finished explaining why her presence was needed at the park, Sandra nervously twisted a silver ring on her finger around and around as her mind took in his words. "Please, no! Don't make me go back to the park. I can draw you a map. I promise I can show you where everything happened." She trembled as she pleaded with investigators. "There must be a map of the park somewhere. Just give me a map, and I can point out anything you want!" She wasn't agitated or angry but rather frightened, though she still managed to speak evenly and without breaking into tears.

"The idea of returning to the park is obviously overwhelming for you, Sandra, and we understand that," Johnson said, speaking with calm authority. "We would not ask you to do this if it weren't absolutely necessary. At some point, everything we find at the park will be used in court, and we need your help to figure out just what happened that night."

"I promise. I can tell you what happened. I just need a map." Sandra shook her head no while looking down at her hands which were folded in her lap.

Johnson glanced at Vinson, who appeared poised to talk.

Vinson paused and softened his voice a bit. "Someday, Sandra, the video of you in the park will be used in a courtroom and will give a vivid and believable picture of what happened the night of the murders. By going out to the park and telling us what happened, you will be helping us solve this terrible crime." He reached over and patted her trembling hand. Then as if letting her in on a secret, he quietly said, "I'm not much of a cook, Sandra, but I sure know how to buy a delicious cup of hot chocolate on the way out to the park. You can do this. Remember when you said you could do whatever it took to help the boys? Now's that time."

Sandra's stomach clenched. She wanted to protest, to run from the room and refuse to return to the hell of Gitchie Manitou. Yet, she began to realize the sheriff was right and it fell on her shoulders to help if she could. The thought of going back to the very spot where the boys took their last breaths seemed unbearable. However, she was no stranger to dealing with life's difficult moments. When Sandra was a child, Lolo had a new man in her life who didn't want to deal with Sandra and her brothers, so he made arrangements for some of the kids to be sent to foster homes. Later, Sandra was shipped off to a Native American boarding school, which in the 1970s was a grim environment. She survived those ordeals, and she'd survive this as well.

Her eyes reluctantly met the investigator's eyes, and at that moment she knew she had to find the courage to go back out. "If it will help the boys," she drew in a slow breath, "I'll do it. I'll do whatever I have to." She sucked in her lip and refused to cry. The boys were brave and she would be brave as well.

Back at Gitchie, several investigators stood before the matted indentation of blood-covered grass. From here, a trail of blood droplets led away from this suspicious spot. The detectives began developing theories. *Did more shooting occur in this location? Had someone died here and been carried away?* The mystery of this matted-down blood stain did not come to light until the case was cracked. After this, nothing but old litter and beer cans were found for the rest of the morning and into the afternoon. In the nearly one-hundred-acre expanse filled with waist-high grasses and naturally terraced, uneven ground, the search inched along unceasingly. At 3 PM a shout arose from one of the lab personnel who found a spent .00 buckshot shell. Shortly after that, the surveyor determined that Roger's body fell in Iowa along with the other boys. Dusk settled in dimming the park, which signaled an end to the day's search. The park tightly concealed its few remaining clues a bit longer.

Chapter 7

November 19, 1973
Sioux Falls, SD & surrounding area

RUMORS ABOUT SOME local kids being murdered rippled through a grapevine of neighborhoods, and when the official news release hit the media on Monday, November 19th, calls clogged the police information line to the point that Johnson assigned Smith to be in charge of leads. Every lead that came through the phone lines was recorded and taken seriously. It was up to Smith to determine the priority of each lead and assign someone to follow up on it. Some information needed to be checked out immediately. Right away, a clerk called in a tip that two males and a female bought shotgun shells at his store on the day of the murders. The detective who followed up went to the store, interviewed the clerk, searched through receipts, spent hours determining the names and addresses of the customers, and interviewed the potential suspects before determining that all had solid alibis at the time of the murders. It was a cold lead that consumed hours of investigative time and was the reason why dozens of lawmen were needed to solve the horrific crime.

Sandra said that the pickup used by the killers was a Chevrolet, and by her unbelievably detailed description, the agents determined it was likely a 1971 model. Some of her extensive recollection included that the glove compartment was narrower at the top than the bottom and had a silver knob that had to be turned and pulled out. "You don't have to press it in like most glove compartments," she noted. She recalled the shape of the speedometer and that the gauges glowed bluish-green in the dark.

The police department was assigned the task of itemizing every pickup in Sioux Falls that matched the description of this vehicle. By morning, the overnight crew printed out a list of every 1971 Chevy pickup in the city. This was without the use of computers and required going through, by hand, filed paper copies of vehicle registrations. Johnson was floored when handed the complete list and a smile of satisfaction crossed Smith's lips when he checked that job off the assignment chart.

"The police here are working their tails off. We're making headway," Smith said. His emphasis on the plural pronoun emphasized the underlying camaraderie that was the wind to the sail of the investigation. He assigned agents to follow up on the owners of the vehicles then turned to the job of sending out detectives to check out locations that sold Smith & Wesson .00 buckshot. They discovered that no one in the area sold this type of ammunition, which led them to wonder from how far away the killers had traveled. Leads rolled in. Then Stew's van was located on the International Truck Sales lot on the north end of Minnesota Avenue in Sioux Falls. Contrary to what the investigators concluded based on the .00 buckshot, this finding led them to speculate that the killers were from the area. Stew's van was processed for latent prints and other physical evidence, which were sent to the crime lab in Des Moines.

CHAPTER 8

November 22, 1973
Lyon County Iowa Sheriff's Department

WHEN AN URGENT CALL from California came in, it sent the case reeling in a different direction. On November 11, two girls, ages twelve and thirteen, were killed by shotguns in a wooded area of Yuba County. Was there a serial killer moving across the country? Calls from across the nation started to pour in from law enforcement agencies trying to determine if the Gitchie murders were related to unsolved crimes in their area. Dealing with all of these calls further strained the resources of the investigators.

Then another disturbing call came in to the Lyon County Sheriff's office. A body, lying in a large pool of blood with a shotgun next to it, was discovered outside of George, Iowa, not far from Gitchie Manitou. Now, the potential for a serial killer was put at the top of the case. Throughout the investigation, Smith formed teams by pairing a local agent who knew the area with a BCI investigator. He sent Steinbeck and Pontius to George, Iowa, to examine a crime scene that revealed a bizarre tale. Since this was also in Lyon County, they met Deputy Griesse at the site. At the same time, Ford was planning a strategy for the upcoming funerals of the four boys.

* * *

A solemnness hung over the investigative detectives on the days of the boys' funerals, which occurred one after another, with three of the funerals on Wednesday due to Thursday being Thanksgiving. The search continued, and leads were followed, but Ford was assigned the task of attending each funeral on the hunch that the murderer or murderers might show up. At each service, he easily blended in with the crowd of mourners. He eagle-eyed his way through the packed crowd, meandering and looking for someone who appeared out of place. There were so many teenagers and young adults that it was difficult to decide if someone didn't fit. From somewhere in the back, organ music began to play, snuffing out the sounds of the packed chapel. Ford continued scanning for anyone suspicious, but it was a diverse group of mourners. The small rooms were packed to capacity with teenage classmates, sobbing and hugging each other, any of whom could have had a connection to the murders. No one stood out, and nothing unusual happened. When Ford returned to the command center, he was informed that Steinbeck and Pontius were headed to George, Iowa, where a body was discovered.

Chapter 9

November 22, 1973
Outside of George, Iowa

THE TWO-STORY HOUSE outside of George, Iowa, appeared uninhabited. The front door hung loose, its rusty screen torn. There were cracked windows caked with grime and one was covered with a piece of worn plywood. The shingles were curled and the weather-worn siding faded and pocked with wood rot. Apart from its appearance, something about this dwelling nestled in a grove of trees struck Agents Steinbeck and Pontius as odd. They stood in a patch of dry leaves noting that the surrounding trees were cut down, or rather it looked as though hacked off, around the perimeter of the house, leaving bare stumps among a swath of overgrown grass and weeds. The two men began with a visual scan of the yard, noted that the felled trees and brush had been cleared away, then peered in each window. A neighbor reported seeing a dead body inside which had possibly been lying there for several days. The place had the makings of a bachelor's house with not much more than essential furnishings and little apparent décor but cluttered with cases of soda bottles and piles of books. They were unable to see anything out of the ordinary through the kitchen window.

The agents entered and observed the kitchen, which smelled of dank mold and something putrid, before continuing on. With each step, a creak billowed from the yellowed linoleum floor. Years of investigating crimes curbed the urge to move directly over to the body, which was located in an entryway below three steps that led to the kitchen. The corpse lay sprawled in a large pool of blood, and random smears indicated that the victim did not die instantly but had thrashed around. At this time, Deputy Griesse pulled up, and after a brief discussion with the other investigators, he went over and talked to a neighboring farmer.

This farmer had taken pity on his nearest neighbor, who was a known recluse, and explained that he brought the man a case of Coca-Cola every week. Today, however, when no one answered the door he peered inside and saw a body lying on the floor. He immediately called the authorities.

This is likely a serial killer related to the Gitchie murders. Griesse shook the farmer's hand, thanked him for the information, and asked to use a phone. They immediately needed lab agents here who were trained to gather evidence without contaminating the site. Griesse wisely avoided using the radio since police scanners were not uncommon among the locals, and he didn't want to risk anyone tampering with the site.

"The nearest phone is in the barn." The farmer motioned with his head, and Griesse walked down a path of matted grass and found the phone just inside the double doors of the barn. In small communities at that time, most homes had a party line, which meant that two or more families shared the same phone line. This inconvenient setup not only limited a person's ability to use their own phone at will if another family happened to already be using the phone, but also allowed for ease of eavesdropping as well. However, the law required that people relinquish the phone lines in the event of an emergency. So, after picking up the receiver a couple of times and determining that this long-winded conversation was nowhere near its end, Griesse lifted the receiver again with no choice but to risk having the talkers listen in on his call. "This is the deputy sheriff, and I need the line for an emergency. Please hang up!" Although there was no doubt in his mind that they did not hang up.

He put a call through to an agent in Sioux Falls, who informed Griesse that "the lab boys just got back to Des Moines and dropped off the evidence from Gitchie."

"Tell them to turn around and come back," Griesse said. "We have another potential murder scene to investigate. I'll give you the details once I'm back at the office." He assumed that once he hung up, phones would begin ringing all through the town.

When he returned to the dead man's house, he entered through a different door rather than through the kitchen to preserve evidence. The investigators kneeled from a short distance away to take a closer look at the smears in the dried blood for clues such as unexplained footprints.

"See that?" Steinbeck pointed toward the top of a wall where dozens of magnets of all sizes were placed. *Odd.* Then he crouched down to get a side view of one of the piles of little bones that littered the top of the counter. Some of the bones had bits of hard, dry gristle that appeared to have been sitting there for some time. The other agent counted several dead starlings next to one of the bone piles. The meat was cut from the birds, and the feathers sat in bunches next to the bone piles. With rancid-tasting meat similar to that of a blackbird, a starling was not something a person would shoot for dinner in the way one might shoot a duck or quail. *What happened to the meat?* He hypothesized it may have been fed to an animal. At that moment, they all saw the most bizarre thing at the same time: three rotting human teeth with the roots attached in a glass of water.

"What the hell happened here?" Steinbeck asked.

Chapter 10

Monday, November 19, 1973 (Continuation)
Gitchie Manitou State Park

Johnson and Vinson zipped up the recording equipment in a leather case. They had in their possession a new Super 8 camera, the latest model with the ability to record sound as well as motion. Off to the side and picking at her nails, a sleep-deprived girl, barely a teenager, had to be slipped out a side door to avoid the media that now pulsed around the perimeter of the building. Although Sandra was exhausted, grieving, and reluctant to return to the park, her video testimony could be crucial in a courtroom. Vinson's calm face conveyed security, which steadied Sandra's nerves.

Sandra had only her light jacket at the detention center. It rippled in the gusty wind that was sweeping across the rolling hills of the park. Johnson and Vinson gave her a few moments to adjust to the shock of seeing the area where her friends had laughed, full of life and not knowing they were about to take their last breaths, just a blink of time earlier. Both men were struck by her fortitude, yet there was concern she might crumble, so Johnson gently began the conversation.

"Sandra, just start from the beginning and tell us what you remember from that night."

She crossed her arms, pulled her coat tight, inhaled, and lightly closed her eyes. The camera rolled, and she told her story, reluctant with shock at first, recalling how she was concerned when the boys were late picking her up in Stew's blue van. She pointed toward the parking area, now bare save for a flutter of leaves skittering across its top.

"We pulled in there, and we got out of the van and went to the shelter."

She pointed toward the covered camp shelter and, along with the two agents, made her way to the structure. On the night of the crimes, the massive blocks of purple granite appeared medieval in the shadowy night when illuminated with nothing but embers from an old fire glowing from within. In fact, it was due to this nearly extinguished fire that the teenagers decided perhaps someone had already claimed this spot and was coming back. The park was a popular gathering place on weekend nights, and it was a distinct possibility that someone might return to the shelter. In fact, it was eerily deserted that Saturday night. Or so it seemed.

The kids walked about seventy yards along a dirt path and built a fire near the river. The scent of wood smoke filled the air while Stew strummed away on the guitar strings until they heard a rustling sound; something was moving through the fallen leaves. It was followed by a swishing, scraping sound. The noises seemed purposeful, like the sounds you might hear from a person brushing against thick bushes and underbrush. The part that spooked them was the fact that the noises approached, stopped, and retreated before starting in all over again. They discussed the unusual sounds, but nervously laughed it off as being afraid of noises in the dark. *"It's probably a bear!"* Roger joked, squeezing Sandra's hand. Her heart beat just a little faster, both thrilled and comforted in the presence of her handsome and capable boyfriend. The fire started to die down, though, and Roger bravely volunteered to gather more branches in the wooded area just beyond the campsite. He kissed Sandra, and right when he reached the tree line the night suddenly spun out of control. Sandra and the agents walked along, and with each step, the leaves crunched, sending up reminders of the ominous footsteps she heard just days before when the boys had stood right here among the backdrop of brown branches and fall-colored paths.

"Just all of a sudden, there were three men standing on that ledge."

She pointed and the camera captured her gesture before scanning the rock ledge that easily could have held three people. Sandra's head went light, and she remembered that the inner radar pulsing in her gut indicated something was terribly wrong. While she spoke, the detectives were able to visualize the full scene of what happened that night.

"The tall, thin man raised his gun, and there was a loud explosion. It echoed and Roger, he just crumpled to the ground."

White smoke and an acrid smell from the gunpowder drifted through the campsite. Before anyone could react, another shot rang out, a flash of light belched from the gun's muzzle, and more gunpowder mingled with the swirls of nighttime fog. In a whirl of chaos, the kids ran in every direction.

"Mike grabbed my arm, jerking me toward a tree and telling me, 'Move, move, move!'"

As she spoke, Sandra walked toward the same tree and was overwhelmed with a feeling of sickness that she forced to the pit of her stomach. She was visibly shaking. The temperature had dropped in the time they'd been out there, but she needed to finish her story, which she did so confidently it almost seemed rehearsed.

"It was just completely quiet, and then we heard Stew yelling, 'Oh, God help me! I'm hurt so bad!' We were scared and confused when we were hiding. We didn't know what to do. Then one of the men started to yell for us to come out with our hands up. He said they were the police. We didn't want to come out. In my head, I was thinking we should run, but Mike said they were police, and we should put our hands up and go out, so we did."

But when the two emerged, Mike asked why the kids were being shot at. The same tall man answered Mike with the blast of a shotgun. Mike spun halfway around and dropped to the ground.

"I fell down next to Mike and tried to play dead. It didn't do any good. They kicked us and made us stand up. Mike was bent over holding his arm because he'd been hit. I looked over, and Dana was also standing by the fire with his hands in the air. I didn't see Roger or Stew, but I could still hear Stew moaning and saying, 'I'm shot! Oh, God, help me!'"

She blinked and wiped the back of one hand across each eyelid. This was the cornerstone of their visit. The investigators needed to know exactly where everyone walked that night in order to hone in on evidence.

"Sneaky had his shotgun and made us all stand with our hands in the air. It was hard for Mike because his arm was hurt."

After that, the three gunmen marched Sandra, Mike, and Dana around the park at gunpoint. The tall man whom the others referred to as the Boss said he was a narcotics officer and even recited a badge number that started with 800. Sandra remembered where he stood when he announced this. Accompanying the Boss was a heavyset man who was periodically called Sneaky and a third assailant with pockmarked cheeks whom they referred to as Hatchet Face. At one point the men ordered the teenagers to stop, and the assailants walked a ways off the trail to discuss something. Mike asked through gritted teeth,

"'Will you call an ambulance, and can we sit down?' But Sneaky said, 'Shut up and stand right where you are.'"

Sneaky's eyes held the threat of death. He stepped back and leveled his shotgun at the kids. Mike went silent.

"Show us where you think they walked," Johnson said, while continuing to write notes. Sandra pointed then paced off the trail where the men had walked to discuss their next move. She quietly continued her story.

"Then Sneaky walked over and asked, 'How many girls are here?'

'Only Sandra,' Mike said."

This answer annoyed Sneaky, who came over, frisked Dana, and took his wallet before walking over to the pickup and checking the boy's ID under the glare of headlights. He grunted then handed the wallet back. While this was going on, the Boss was rummaging around in the pickup and returned with a spool of gray wire.

> "The Boss said, 'We don't have handcuffs with us, so I'm going to tie your hands with this.' He turned me around and wrapped the wire around my wrists. He said, 'And don't fight it. This wire will cut the hell out of you.'"

The cold of the wire heightened her senses, and she could feel that it would indeed slice skin if she struggled. Then he locked his arms around her small frame and lifted her into the front seat of the pickup. He smelled of body odor and cigarettes. Sandra watched him reach for something on the floorboard, and he came up with a gunnysack, which he proceeded to put over her head, even with Sandra desperately trying to squirm away.

> "I begged him, 'Please take it off! Take it off me!'"

And for whatever reason, the Boss did. He shook his head and threw the sack back on the floorboard. He got behind the wheel and coasted down the dirt path that led out of the park. Sandra turned to look out the back window and saw the boys standing at gunpoint at the hands of Sneaky and Hatchet Face. She locked eyes with Dana until the truck turned, and her friends disappeared in a haze. Sandra's voice cracked.

> "The boys were so brave, but they had such sad looks on their faces. It made my heart sink."

Sandra became emotionally shaken and was shivering with cold. "That's enough for out here. Let's head back," Vinson said with the same compassionate voice that Sandra had come to trust. She had walked them everywhere the kids and killers were that dreadful night, and the information she provided proved to be invaluable. Vinson instinctively understood she needed a break before divulging details of the sexual assault and what happened after leaving the park.

Chapter 11

November 21, 1973
Sioux Falls, SD

WHEN AGENTS FORD and Smith conducted their interview with Sandra on November 21, Ford found her recollection of details remarkable. When asked whether any of the men wore jewelry, she recalled that the tall man wore a watch. When asked to describe it, she replied, "Well, it was kind of an old one, it wasn't new and it...had a band on it, one like when you pull them apart they come back together and stretch."

"I can't envision how a thirteen-year-old could have that bearing," he remarked after the meeting. Smith agreed. "Some of the elements have no logic," he added, honing in on a collective bewilderment over The Boss supposedly dropping her off at her house after the murders. Their underlying inclination was that something was "off," and indeed it was.

Additionally, a concerning fact emerged. Sandra claimed that The Boss verbally offered his badge number as proof that he was a narcotics agent. The number he supplied started with 800, but she couldn't remember the other two digits. At that moment, Ford and Smith both paused and looked at each other with unease. They knew that in Iowa, narcotics agents were assigned badge numbers in the 800s, and it led the team to explore the possibility that corrupt cops might have been involved in the murders. It was a point of such significance that they immediately telephoned the drug division in the Des Moines headquarters to see if any drug agents had been placed near Gitchie, perhaps as an undercover assignment.

The thought of this gave them both a prickle of hope as well as dread. Their intense desire for a lead was overshadowed by the thought that they might discover it was one of their own, a law enforcement agent who was involved in the slaughter. However unpalatable it was to consider the involvement of a law enforcement agent in the crime, their dedication to bringing justice trumped their dedication to a potentially dirty brother in blue. Both of them shifted with uneasy tension during the time it took a supervisor to check the location of each drug division member near the time of the murders. Ford and Smith's demeanor improved noticeably upon finding out that no one in the bureau was stationed near Gitchie at the time in question. As much of a relief as that was, it meant another cold lead.

There were other explanations for the 800 number, however. It could have been a random number but likely not. They knew that people tend to be drawn back to something in their memory bank, and their hunch was that the number carried importance. For a criminal, the number might have been a prison number that he used to impersonate a narcotics agent instead, which turned out to be an uncannily accurate hunch.

Chapter 12

**November 1973 (Continuation)
Outside of George, Iowa**

HUMAN TEETH IN A GLASS of water. A body in a pool of dried blood. Bird bones and carcasses with the meat gnawed away lying on the kitchen counter. Magnets hanging all over a dilapidated house. Trees hacked down to stumps in a circle around this bizarre dwelling outside of George, Iowa. The scene had the investigators baffled. They dug deeper into the mystery and determined what had transpired.

The acreage was owned by a man who was a known recluse. He shot starlings and blackbirds for his primary food source, and a neighbor brought him a case of Coca-Cola every week. The man would not leave the house to go to a dentist, so when his teeth rotted, he pulled them with a pair of pliers and placed them in glasses of water. On an even more peculiar note, he believed that the Germans were going to invade, so he hung magnets of all shapes and sizes around the house to throw off the radar of the enemy planes. He cut down the trees around his property so Germans couldn't hide behind them when they invaded.

Determining how the shooting occurred was more difficult. The shotgun found next to him had gone off, but only a few BBs had entered the man's body. One of these hit his carotid artery. While the blood slowly pulsed out, the man evidently became weak and began thrashing around in the blood. They developed two theories based on the evidence. One was that the man committed a rather botched suicide. The second theory was that he slipped or fell, causing the gun to discharge. He was found in the entryway leading to the kitchen, which struck them as an odd location for a suicide. Further investigation revealed that it was a botched suicide attempt. The man placed the butt of the shotgun on one of the steps and stood above the barrel, which he placed in his mouth. When he reached down to pull the trigger, the barrel pulled away from his mouth, but three or four BBs caused enough damage that he bled to death. Of greatest importance to the case, however, was that it was not related to the incident at Gitchie Manitou but rather was another cold lead.

Chapter 13

November 21, 1973
South Dakota State Penitentiary, Sioux Falls, SD

FORD WAS ASSIGNED the job of going to the state penitentiary to look at all of the 800 prison numbers and the accompanying mug shots. For Ford, the scope of the entire investigation was more overwhelming than he expected. Although new to the BCI, he spent six years as a state trooper. He was used to investigating traffic accidents and routine crimes for which he developed the necessary coping mechanism of a first responder, which was to remove his emotions when investigating a crime scene. This assignment, however, required the precise skill of being able to focus on examining these prison files with an almost obsessive perseverance. Ford quickly found he had a natural knack for thoroughness and attention to detail.

Fortunately, the penitentiary was only a few miles away. An imposing structure of thick Sioux quartzite, the color of the massive building changed from pink to purple to dark gray depending on the angle of the sun. Inside the records department, Ford loosened his tie and removed his double-knit sport coat. He scrutinized nearly one hundred folders for inmates with prison numbers in the 800s and eliminated those people who were deceased or still incarcerated, as well as those whose picture in no way matched the description of the killers based on advanced age or ethnicity. In several instances, the mug shot was missing from the file; he made it a priority to follow up on the files with missing photos. In the end, Ford walked away with the files for several potential suspects that he was eager to track down to determine their whereabouts on the night of the murders.

That morning, Johnson and Vinson arranged a meeting packed with BCI agents, Sioux Falls detectives and deputies, and every law enforcement agent who might be associated with solving the case. The air already bristled with tension, a result of increasing public pressure to solve the murders.

Johnson strode toward the podium and briefed the group with updated information. Everyone in the room appeared receptive to his leadership, yet there was the unmistakable sensation of frustration as well. The number of cold leads continued to escalate. The media clamored for information. The public demanded answers. Before speaking, Johnson paused and made a quick scan of the room, something he did both regularly and automatically as an intense observer of people.

"Our next step is to discuss the strategies we'll use to catch the suspects. Our number one order of business is how do we identify the murderers?"

After that there was a heated discussion about various theories based on Sandra's information that the men claimed to be narcotics agents. Johnson led the discussion back on course.

"Does this ring a bell? Do you know of any citizens who've been arrested for trying this tactic of impersonating an agent in the past?" Johnson asked, but no one was aware of such a thing, so he pressed for more information. "We know that if someone gets ripped off on a drug deal, they don't run to the police. Could these killings be in retaliation for some situation with drugs? Keep in mind your well-known dealers, and it might lead us to some suspects."

There were some murmurs and sidebar discussions, but his theory hit a brick wall. No one had any useful information. It became apparent early in the investigation that Johnson possessed the trifecta of traits required of a lead investigator: patience, the ability to analyze deeply, and a creative imagination. Johnson learned to become a winner from a young age. In high school he was a standout football player on an iconic team with an enviable record. So he never developed a taste for losing and didn't intend on starting now. In spite of the respect he garnered, the unasked question dangling in the air was, *Now which direction do we go?* Johnson decided that they would start where Sandra remembered going the night of the murders.

Sandra was brought to the command center for another interview. The reason for the repeated interviews they conducted was twofold. First, a different investigator might be able to glean additional information, and every clue regardless of its size was vital. Secondly, they compared the interviews to note discrepancies. A witness who is making up a story tends to add, change, and embellish with each retelling. They led Sandra into one of the interview rooms that was allotted specifically for the Gitchie investigation.

The small room with its fluorescent overhead lighting, bare walls, and sparse furnishings did nothing to create warmth or comfort for Sandra, who once again mentally prepared herself to relive the events of the sickening night. She was at first reluctant to talk to yet another new person. Her mom came for emotional support, and although she was not allowed in the interview room, she was just down the hall, which gave Sandra comfort. Sandra explained again about driving down seemingly endless gravel and blacktop roads with The Boss after leaving the boys standing there in the park.

"I don't have any idea where we were or what direction we traveled. It was my first time going to the park, and it was so dark." She recounted driving down a long driveway and to a red gas tank behind a house that appeared to be on a farm. The Boss mentioned that as an undercover agent, he had keys for gas tanks all over the state and could fill up wherever he wanted as long as he left ten dollars. The Boss backed out and went further down the road to an abandoned house, where she was raped by Sneaky. To Agent Smith, her story made sense except that it struck him as peculiar in spots. He kept an open mind while remaining perplexed that one of the murderers suddenly decided to bring her home.

"She seems thick-skinned for someone who's thirteen," he noted to Ford in the no-nonsense way that was typical of Smith. "But she is both frank and honest in my opinion." However, not everyone on the team agreed with his analysis.

Chapter 14

November 22, 1973
Sioux Falls, SD

FORD WAS ONE of the first BCI agents to rotate out of his assignment for a quick trip home primarily to wash and pack more clothes. He spent a few hours with his wife and two young sons before heading back on Thanksgiving morning. Spending holidays without his family went with the job. Several of the agents went home with Detective Ed Flowers from Sioux Falls for a hearty meal then spent the rest of the day on paperwork. Four days later, Johnson turned thirty years old, a day he barely had time to acknowledge. The only gift he wished for was to crack the case. He readied himself for daily briefings with his supervisors in Des Moines. If a new tip looked promising, he called them two or three times a day due to the seriousness of the crimes. Generally, they offered encouragement.

"You guys can get this done," they often told Johnson, though it was part of his personality, always had been, not to stop until every wrinkle had been smoothed from the fabric of the investigation.

"What about the lead on that vehicle Steinbeck was following up on in Mitchell, South Dakota?" Stump asked. Johnson imagined his boss carefully paging through a binder of meticulous notes.

"Well, that washed out," Johnson reported. It seemed that tip after tip after tip fell through. After hanging up the receiver, he looked around the office, content that it was bustling with productivity, then shut the door behind him and found an empty room for further frustrating reflection.

CHAPTER 15

November 23, 1973
Sioux Falls, SD

IN A CITY WHERE typical headlines heralded a new school being built or a sold-out concert at the Arena, people clamored for details on the latest developments regarding the murders of four of their own. The shocking story attracted determined journalists and news crews from across the tri-state area, and many staked out near the police department in order to track agents following up on leads and to ask questions of law enforcement officials who paraded in and out of the building. Of high interest was getting photos and video of Sandra, which resulted in the investigators having to use every precaution to keep Sandra's whereabouts unidentified. She was in perpetual danger until the killers were caught. If the media was parked out front, they slipped Sandra in through the back door. One day proved particularly challenging. Vinson picked up Sandra at Steinbeck's request and radioed ahead to the police department to determine where they should enter.

"It must be a slow day for the media," Ford replied. "The building is surrounded by cameras."

"Do you have your vehicle parked there?" Vinson asked, to which Ford replied that he did. The two came up with a brilliant plan to throw the media off their scent. It was one they successfully used several times throughout the course of the investigation. Ford hung up the phone, ran out the front door, hustled to his official car, and hopped in. He checked both side mirrors and raced away from the curb before flipping on the red lights. With the media in hot pursuit, he drove with urgency, yet didn't speed, out to Gitchie Manitou. Upon arriving, Ford exited the car with a serious expression. Cameras flashed. He looked around, eventually picked up a random object from the ground which he placed in his pocket, got back in the vehicle, and returned to the police station.

During that time, Steinbeck smuggled Sandra into the station and had her describe the farm where she told them she was taken and raped. Across the table, Steinbeck scribbled as Sandra spoke. He adjusted, erased, and continued to draw until what he created matched her descriptions.

"Go over every detail you can remember about this abandoned farm," he directed.

A broken-down fence. A house with a dilapidated porch. Shattered and boarded up windows. Outbuildings that leaned with age. Her descriptions were meticulous. Steinbeck was struck with the indescribable terror she must have felt there in the black of night with a stranger looming over her shoulder while she peered in the dark window of an abandoned house in the middle of nowhere. He was also puzzled by the fact that certain elements of the story simply did not match with common sense. He didn't disbelieve her but considered that she might not be recalling how everything happened perhaps due to trauma. He repeated the process for another farm where The Boss stopped to fill up the truck from a red gas tank. Sandra looked at the drawings and nodded her head in approval. Before Ford returned from his fictitious emergency, Sandra was returned to the detention center.

Copies of the sketches were made and distributed to detectives, investigators, sheriffs, police officers, and state troopers. They were not going to wait for someone to simply stumble upon the farm, however. Along with the drawings, they developed a map in the form of a circular grid covering a fifty-mile radius around Sioux Falls. Based on Sandra's recollection of how far they traveled that night, it was determined that the location could be anywhere in this massive expanse of land. To avoid overlapping the same roads, the grid was prepared in a 360-degree layout and broken into the areas of Lyon, Lincoln, and Minnehaha counties. When an area was searched, it was marked off. Anyone who located an abandoned farm that resembled the description called in the location, and Sandra was driven to the property to ascertain whether she remembered this being where The Boss had taken her.

From dawn to dusk every day, the search ambled on while agents covered countless miles of dusty gravel roads and stretches of blacktop highways. On numerous occasions, Sandra was driven to an abandoned farm with high hopes, only to have another letdown as the teenage girl hung her head and reluctantly told them, "This isn't the place." Each time she felt as if she were letting them down once again. All the way there and back, she scanned the sides of the road with both anticipation and anxiety that she might actually identify the repulsive farm and give some additional traction to the investigation.

CHAPTER 16

**Late November 1973
Sioux Falls, SD**

THE AROMA OF COFFEE percolating drifted through the room that was filling up with men wearing suits and carrying briefcases. Every officer and agent involved in the case gathered for a daily meeting. Johnson informed them of new developments and discussed which leads needed to be followed up that day. After the meeting dispersed, a few agents sat around a Formica table sipping from Styrofoam cups. Though it was early morning, they already faced an insurmountable number of tasks to complete.

One of the veteran homicide detectives pulled up a chair next to his partner, who had opened a folder. "You know what I think?" he said while scanning some paperwork through bloodshot eyes. "This girl is feeding us a line of crap." Many of the detectives were thinking that from the start, and now this commonly held sentiment was being whispered throughout the station.

The rational explanation and truth must lie somewhere between the young girl's story and logical patterns associated with murder. The investigators needed to dig and pry to find the truth if Sandra was indeed lying. They focused on the parts she may have left out. A mass murder by complete strangers is extremely rare, and then the claim that The Boss drove this girl home and dropped her off gave rise to even more suspicion.

"She could be protecting a person of interest," one of them suggested.

"A boyfriend perhaps," someone else added. "It could have been a jealous boyfriend who followed her out there and saw her with another guy."

"We can't overlook the question of why she wasn't killed following the rape."

Johnson's calls to headquarters became more frequent when no clear suspects emerged. The pressure deepened. Johnson had already lost ten pounds. He rubbed his temples and blocked out the tapping of keys on a nearby typewriter. His supervisors were supportive but made no bones about their expectations. He'd been in charge of demanding cases before but none as intensive as this. He remained focused, the way he had in college where athletes were required to play two sports. Johnson chose wrestling with the thinking that he'd be conditioned after a season of football. His first practice on the mat proved otherwise, but instead of giving up he worked harder. In spite of the intense pressure and sleepless nights, he loved the satisfaction that came with solving a crime and scoring a point on the side of justice. When a call came from Des Moines, Johnson noticed an unfamiliar edge to his supervisor's tone.

"We want you to stay in touch with us, and we will give you the help you need, but you have to get it done."

On November 27th, the Minnehaha Sheriff's Office, the state patrol, and the Lincoln County Sheriff's Office searched the entire northern half of Lincoln County. At the same time, the Lyon County Sheriff's Office, along with agents from the Iowa Beer and Liquor Division, conducted an extensive search of farms in Lyon County, Iowa. Each day more agencies were called upon to help sort through and investigate the mounding leads.

"You are wasting time, money, and manpower driving that grid on a wild goose chase for a farm that doesn't exist! Give it a few more days, and that girl will eventually tire of her ruse and tell us who was involved," one cynical detective harangued Steinbeck several days into the grid search.

Then the door opened, and an agent walked in holding up a slip of paper.

"We've received a tip, and it's somewhat strange. We can't figure out how this note got here, and I think Smith will want to take a look at it right away. Do you know where he is?"

Chapter 17

November 26, 1973
Sioux Falls, SD Police Department

WHILE SMITH WAS BEING located to view the mysterious note, Sandra was facing more strife. Due to the controversy regarding her story, which was riddled with somewhat unbelievable claims, it was decided that she would be given a polygraph test. To the surprise of many, she passed. However, more interviews were scheduled, in part to see if her story stayed consistent.

Inside a small room of the temporary headquarters for the Gitchie case, investigators prepared to talk with Sandra again. When led into the nearly bare room, she appeared quiet yet composed, glancing at the detectives as if anticipating what was about to transpire. They explained that she needed to tell everything she could remember from the night of the murders and emphasized the importance of details, a matter on which Sandra did not disappoint.

"Can you describe the men?"

"One was sort of tall. He had a hat on, the kind like farmers wear with little flaps sticking out. He was carrying a shotgun."

"How old was this man?"

"He was in his thirties. I'm not sure. He said, 'I'm old enough to be your dad.'"

"What color hair did he have?"

"Dark brown or black."

"Did he have a mustache?"

"No."

"Was there anything about his teeth or nose or face that you recall?"

"His teeth were all crooked, and I think he had blue eyes."

"How would you describe the other man?"

Sandra went on to describe Hatchet Face as being about twenty-nine years old, slim, and about five feet nine inches. He was shorter than The Boss, had blond hair, wore a cap, jeans, and a jean jacket. He had a shotgun, but she did not see him fire it. The third man she described as being heavyset with short brown hair and a thin mustache. She thought he was wearing blue jeans and was also about twenty-nine years old and five feet seven inches.

She said that at one point, The Boss pulled to the side of the road and put the truck in park. He narrowed his eyes at Sandra and sternly announced that he was going to make another drug raid that night. Then Sandra proceeded to tell about another claim he made. "He said the Hells Angels were sitting in the desert in

California with a campfire like ours except they put marijuana on it, and you could smell it for miles around. The Boss said when he tried to bust them, they had knives, and it was a hard fight." The Boss claimed he was paid $2,000 per week for his services.

Then she told about arriving at the abandoned house and what transpired. The other two assailants soon showed up in a small, light-colored car. "After Hatchet Face and Sneaky left the old farm, what occurred?" The agent's voice took on a more serious tone.

"The Boss said, 'I'm going to take you in that old house and try to scare you to death.' And he was going, 'Boo! Boo!' He took a wood piece off the pickup floor. It looked like the handle of an axe, and he took me over to the old house with a flashlight. We looked in the broken windows, but it was so creepy I almost screamed." Sandra's voice cracked. She started to tear up but suppressed the emotions. She told the agents that The Boss would definitely have killed her with the wooden handle had she gone in the abandoned house. "I ran back to the pickup and got in. He said he would take me home and kept telling me if I told anyone that he would sure get me. He stopped by our mailbox and wanted my phone number. He told me he would put the number in his little black book and call me. I went into the house. It was five o'clock."

"Five o'clock AM? Morning?"

"Yes, and I went in and told my brother what had happened."

Sandra swallowed hard, and though trembling, she began reliving memories she preferred to bury. During the first interview, Sioux Falls police detective Skadsen and Sheriff Vinson did not press for details about the rape from Sandra. Finally the time came when they needed all the information about what transpired that night, and when asked about Sneaky entering the pickup, Sandra's face withered. She gazed into her hands but did not refuse to answer. In a quiet but steady voice she told about The Boss getting out of the pickup and walking away with Hatchet Face. When Sneaky slid into the driver's seat he had a strange look on his face.

"He scared me, and I wanted to jump out of the truck and run, but I couldn't move. He started touching me. He leaned in with this evil look on his face."

Sneaky ordered Sandra to remove her clothing.

"I must not have been taking my clothes off fast enough because he starting pulling them off of me."

He yanked her pants down with no regard for the trembling girl inside of them, and then raped her violently; Sandra's head slammed into the door handle. Her lungs could hardly take in air. His heavy body crushed her. And then came the bizarre feeling that she was looking down on herself as if it were all happening to someone else. She wasn't able to theorize that her subconscious had removed her from the event.

"I started thinking that the girls at school won't believe this when I tell them on Monday." It was a surreal thought and one that she was later embarrassed to admit. After a few minutes, he removed himself from on top of her. Even though she was disgusted, she was instantly thankful that it was over. He stepped out of the vehicle with his pants down. A few moments later, she noticed her rumpled jeans and underwear on the floorboard but closed her eyes and looked away. The thought of moving her hand to pick them up seemed a feat requiring more effort than she could muster. An involuntary sigh rose from somewhere within her, though she wasn't sure from where. Her body no longer seemed to belong to her. It took several minutes for her to find the strength to re-dress. She sat in silence until the driver's door opened and The Boss climbed in.

"That wasn't so bad, was it?" he asked with a smirk on his face.

But it was worse than bad, and inside, the old Sandra started to alter. It was the aftermath of being an innocent child one moment and then being forever changed in just a few minutes. She hung her head, something that was not in her nature, and choked out four words, "I was a virgin." But The Boss didn't believe her.

"No you weren't," he said coldly.

Tears burned in the corners of Sandra's eyes, but she held them back; she wouldn't give him that satisfaction.

Chapter 18

November 24, 1973
Lyon County, Iowa Sheriff's Department

SHERIFF VINSON'S OFFICE was flooded with calls, including inquiries from NBC in New York and media outlets from California to the East Coast. It became overwhelming, but Vinson and Griesse stayed focused on finding the killers. In the midst of this, a tip came in regarding two newly hired police officers in northwest Iowa as potential suspects in the case. Vinson made some preliminary calls based on the scanty information he had. He found out that the two were fanatical about sharing their disapproval of illicit drugs and favored the use of drug raids, which was a term "The Boss" used the night Sandra was kidnapped. The parallels did not end there. Vinson asked for and received a description of each officer. His interest was piqued when he learned their descriptions matched two of the assailants. Just beyond the hallway was a row of jail cells, and the typical rise of conversations and slightly chaotic clatter tumbled in through the doorway. He stayed alert for any noise out of the ordinary.

"Do you have any knowledge of what they drive for their personal vehicles?" Vinson asked the police captain on the other end of the phone. He listened for the answer then replied, "Can you bring them in? I'll be there in two hours." He hung up the receiver and let out a heavy sigh. His only deputy had returned minutes ago from investigating an accident on a country road and looked up from the report he was writing in the same cramped room. Griesse would once again have to add a few extra hours onto his workload today to pick up the slack left by Vinson's required presence in the investigation. Both men had worked from the minute they woke up until they collapsed into bed at night and would continue to do so until the suspects were in custody. The daily requirements for running a jail and answering calls throughout an entire county did not stop for them.

"Can you believe it?" Vinson said with unease. "One of the officers owns a small, light-colored vehicle and the other one a pickup." It was one of the most promising leads to date yet at the same time was marred by the possibility they might be investigating dirty cops.

Vinson met with the two suspects individually. As would be expected, the anxiety level swelled in these young officers as the interviews progressed and each realized the purpose of the meeting. Following the questioning, he cross-checked their stories, and all suspicions faded. Despite the numerous coincidences, both cops had solid alibis on the night of the Gitchie murders. Once again, an entire afternoon was devoted to following up on a lead that went cold, but Vinson was relieved and chalked it up to the diligence necessary to solve any crime.

* * *

When Smith arrived back at the BCI command center, he read the mysterious note that was handed to him.

"Where did this come from?" He was bewildered.

The agent shrugged. "It's odd. This office area was completely locked up when we went to dinner, but when we came back, it had been slipped under an inner door."

"Who would have keys to get to this inner area other than someone from the police department or the BCI? But why would an officer need to sneak a note under a door, and what would make someone suspect this individual?" Smith responded.

Again, he glanced down at the slip of paper, which read *"Check into James Fryer as one of the killers."*

"Does anyone from the department recognize the name James Fryer?" Smith asked, to which the agent replied that no one did.

Smith picked up a notebook and added "check into James Fryer" to the list of tips that had not yet been followed up. In the end, it was never determined who put this foretelling note under the door.

Chapter 19

November 29, 1973
Sioux Falls, SD Police Department

THE 29TH OF NOVEMBER marked the twelfth day of the intense search for the truth behind the Gitchie murders. With each passing day, pressure from the community, news media, and BCI supervisors squeezed in on the team of investigators working relentlessly out of the Sioux Falls Police Department. They had interviewed nearly 125 people, some more than once. Though it was well known throughout the BCI that Deputy Director Stump had a fear of flying, he nonetheless contacted the Des Moines agency's pilot and hopped aboard a state-owned single prop plane for a white-knuckle trip to Sioux Falls.

Stump's presence signaled the seriousness of the investigation's perceived lack of significant progress. Stump ultimately bore the outcome of the entire investigation and, after arriving by plane, was in a thoroughly foul mood. It went unspoken that his time was more valuable than most. He gathered a group of police officers, detectives, and BCI agents, including Johnson, Ford, Steinbeck, and Smith, into a debriefing room that quivered with unease when Stump made a grand entrance. He was a cop's cop: tall, fit, and sharply dressed in a dark suit. The flecks of gray in his hair gave a look of experience. Stump got along better with some more than others, which typically depended on how he viewed their job performance. A man who did his job efficiently would fall under Stump's good graces. His ability to determine who was valuable, combined with not hesitating to come down on an agent who was slacking off, led to Stump being held in high regard as a leader. Yet in spite of his seriousness, it was widely accepted that for the most part his bark was worse than his bite; his harsh words were his way of conveying high expectations and reminding everyone who was in charge.

The conversations quickly evaporated. After flipping through a few pages of notes, he addressed the audience. "There has been a tremendous amount of work done here." Stump glanced down at an impressively large binder of notes he carried with him. "You've shown diligence in following up on some promising leads," he said, meeting their eyes with unflinching determination. He was thorough in giving credit where it was due, while making it obvious that only solving the case would bring complete satisfaction. "Bring me up to speed on what has transpired since we last spoke."

Johnson summarized the latest investigation findings to his supervisor, who stood with folded arms and a serious look on his chiseled face. Stump wordlessly scribbled a few notes before looking up again and speaking with conviction. He gave a long and rather hard-nosed pep talk and ended by saying in a more powerful voice, "Gentlemen, your work here is not over until you catch someone. It's gone on long enough. I understand what you're up against, but this is serious. You can all stay here until hell freezes over if that's how long it takes. I can have your paychecks mailed here, but here you *will* stay until the investigation is closed!"

Stump remained stone-faced. When he spoke, his underlings listened. To get on the wrong side of this powerful man served no one well. Tension weighted the air. Johnson's emotions churned, but he kept the feelings inside and maintained professional stoicism. He didn't need anyone to tell him to get it done and perhaps took the tongue-lashing a bit more personally than the others. It took Smith to break the thick silence.

"You know, sir, if we can stop eating up valuable time with these meetings, maybe we could make progress out in the field and get this solved," he said with his characteristic approach of being direct. The others shifted uncomfortably in their chairs. Smith's inclination proved to be uncannily accurate. In an attempt to ward off backlash from Smith's remark, one of the agents cleared his throat and then interjected.

"Sir, let's all get back to work and get it done, and you might want to get in the air to head back to Des Moines before dark when flying is more dangerous."

This ploy at Stump's fear of flying worked. The director paged through his notes in silence for several seconds before turning to the group as he walked out the door. "I'll be in touch," he said sternly. With that, the tension melted away, and after a few wisecracks regarding the meeting, the agents went their separate ways with Smith announcing, "I need fresh air." He decided to head northwest of Sioux Falls to follow up on a recent lead. Earlier that day a group of agents surveying an area of the grid spotted an abandoned farm that matched Steinbeck's drawing. Smith, along with a few others, collected Sandra to go view the site. While they made the thirty-minute drive there, Stump's plane headed back to Des Moines.

When Sandra saw the abandoned farm, she shook her head and said, "No," in a listless tone. She stared out the window at the stubble cornfields and skeletal trees. The empty search for the farm left her feeling as barren as the surrounding cropland. It began to seem that the hunt for this farm was like looking for the proverbial needle in a haystack. After all she did—gave written accounts, had three interviews, helped create sketches of the killers and the crime scene, went back to the site of the murders, and was removed from her home—she was running on fumes. The only thing that kept her going was the determination to seek justice for her four friends.

She was concentrating on the farms whizzing by one after the other, all looking familiar in some way but none matching the place they were looking for, when suddenly Sandra perked up and leaned toward her window. "I think *that's* the farm right there!" The car jerked with a sharp tap on the brakes then slowed and eased down a rutted lane that led to the abandoned farm Sandra spotted.

"Yes, this is it!" Sandra said.

In another amazing stroke of luck, a pickup truck came coasting down the road. Sandra let out a bloodcurdling scream, "THAT'S HIM! THAT'S HIM! THAT'S THE BOSS!" She grabbed Agent Smith, frantically clutching onto him for protection.

In that moment, Sandra's description of the pickup truck with its cracked window driven by a tall, thin driver tooling past the abandoned farm came to life with stunning accuracy. Allen "The Boss" Fryer, age twenty-nine, was detained, and throughout this, Sandra cried hysterically. The agents knew they had to get her away from there immediately and get her back to the detention center. They radioed for BCI agents Richard Searle and Dennis Smith to come to the scene and transport Sandra back to Sioux Falls. While en route, she began to calm down by focusing within. "Is my mascara running?" she asked. They reassured her that she looked fine, and at the detention center, brought her directly to the counselor's office for yet another brief statement to corroborate the details of what occurred prior to Allen's apprehension.

At the farm, Smith got into Allen's pickup with him before the official arrest. There was a shotgun on the floorboard, so Smith put his foot on it and made a quick scan of the cab. There were all the details Sandra described so accurately: the inspection sticker, the crack in the windshield, a gun rack. Smith turned and locked eyes with Allen in a silent stand-off.

"He knew that I knew, and I knew that he knew that I knew," Smith later said wryly.

Suddenly Allen reached under his shirt to his belt and Smith's hand flew to his own .357 revolver, thinking Allen was going for a gun. However, Allen pulled a pack of Pall Malls out of his belt, and Smith let out an audible sigh. Never before had he known anyone to keep their cigarettes in a belt.

The vindication felt by those who believed Sandra from the beginning turned into exaltation. But not for long. Sioux Falls Detective Ed Flowers and BCI agent Tim McDonald arrived at the abandoned farm to transport Allen to the Sioux Falls Police Department for a detailed interview. His version of what happened that night contradicted all of Sandra's claims and threatened to turn the investigation inside out.

Johnson tightened his belt another notch that morning before leaving the Holiday Inn. His appetite all but disappeared at the onset of the investigation. They were all working sixteen-hour days or longer. Smith's call reporting Allen's identification did not result in the workload tapering off. On the contrary, the intensity of the case switched gears and the team did not sleep or rest for the next thirty-six hours. Johnson worked to expedite the flow of tasks: search for weapons, find out where the suspects had been and who'd they'd been with, obtain search warrants, search physical property, and most importantly, find and arrest two more suspects. The investigation scattered in multiple directions but with control and purpose; they were a small army taking position. While Allen was in the process of being transported to Sioux Falls, Smith and the Minnehaha Sheriff's Department worked to get permission to immediately secure and search the farm and to have Allen's truck towed and impounded.

Chapter 20

November 29, 1973
Sioux Falls, SD Police Department

ON NOVEMBER 29TH at 5:40 PM, almost two weeks after the murders, Allen Fryer was read his rights just yards from the abandoned house where he had originally planned to kill Sandra. One of the agents stayed behind to interview the manager of the property as well as get his permission to search the premises. Another group of investigators sped out there to assist in searching for evidence.

Nearly every person associated with the case was assigned a job related to this satisfying break in the investigation. Johnson poured another cup of coffee and steeled himself for an investigative marathon. It often surprised people unfamiliar with law enforcement that as much police work happens after a case is cracked as before.

The first order of business was to question Allen, a farmhand who was married and had two stepdaughters. Allen was advised of his rights and informed that he'd been identified as a suspect in the Gitchie Manitou murders. Johnson's adrenaline kicked in, which was fortunate considering the enormous workload that lay ahead before he or any of the investigators would be rewarded the luxury of sleep.

Johnson and Detective Flowers proceeded to conduct the first interview with Allen Fryer. At 7:00 PM, Allen was ushered into a small but comfortable, well-lit room and again read his Miranda rights before signing a statement acknowledging that he understood his rights and was willing to talk. Rather than appearing noticeably nervous, Allen was cheerful and cooperative. The carefree demeanor hid the evil deviant who lurked beneath his good-ol'-boy act. Wearing jeans, a jean jacket, and a work shirt, he immediately came across as friendly and approachable. Johnson motioned for Allen to sit on the opposite chair. Allen removed his blue Sokota seed cap, patted it, and said, "This is my baby!" Then he began telling his version of what transpired on November 17th.

At about 8:30 or 9 PM, he stopped at the Buffalo Trading Post and spent $11.75 on tickets for a raffle, since the prize was a hunting rifle he desired. He then purchased $5.00 worth of gas for his truck and stayed until sometime between 11:00 and 11:45 PM, noting that he was the only one there besides the employee. Next, they discussed why Allen was driving past the abandoned place where law enforcement stopped him. Allen said he worked for the person who manages the farm. The manager directed him to check out the cars around the abandoned farm buildings because they had previous grain thefts and often found litter from parties being held there. He was checking it out when the authorities stopped him. His story took an unexpected turn when Allen started telling a tale about a friend named Bill who owned a red pickup truck and who had conveniently just moved away. Allen was adamant that he considered Bill a key suspect. Allen suspiciously didn't know

Bill's last name, but he described him as "five feet, eleven inches tall and a hundred fifty-five pounds with dark hair." It quickly became apparent that Allen was hoping to steer the suspicion onto someone else.

Later one of the investigators commented, "I think Allen described Bill as himself. Same height. Same weight. Same color hair and owns a pickup!" They were unmoved by Allen's attempts to shift the blame to "Bill."

"Now Allen, describe *your* pickup," Johnson directed gently. It was a widely known rule not to get angry or get a suspect ticked off in the first interview because the subject would likely clam up.

"It's a blue 1971 Chevy, and had a rack on it 'til about three weeks ago," Allen said, referring to the livestock rack he'd put on to haul hogs to market for his boss. They never did take the hogs to market, so he eventually removed the rack.

Johnson nodded, careful to muzzle his emotion at this point. "Let's take a quick break. Would you like a cup of coffee?" Allen responded, "Yes," and seemed relieved to have the opportunity to reconfigure his story. Johnson recorded a seemingly menial note that they took a break at 7:45 PM and gave him food, not knowing that this act would prove vital in a shocking legal maneuver years down the road.

The detectives weren't taking a break. One of them slipped away to the phone and made contact with the employee at the Trading Post. The others were strategizing a plan. When they reconvened with Allen at 8:25 PM, Johnson broke the news to him.

"Your story doesn't match," he said, leaning in toward Allen with authority before proceeding to tell Allen that he checked with the Trading Post. Johnson also pointed out that Allen's truck matched the description they were given, and he was identified by a witness. Allen went quiet.

"What was your penitentiary number, Allen?" Johnson asked firmly.

"Eight-one-two," he replied, with a bit of cockiness, apparently not realizing the importance of this information.

The investigators looked at each other and Johnson gave a confident nod. Their hunch was correct. Allen used his prison number when he told Sandra he was a narcotics agent and that his badge number was 812. Ford later determined after going through the prison numbers that Allen's file had been one that did not have a mug shot included. It was in the group that he was following up on for photos and information but had not yet gotten to Allen's.

Emboldened by their progress, Johnson called another break after only twenty minutes to take a call from the BCI Deputy Director, Stump. "Congratulations, and tell the others nice work," Stump said in a tone that relayed satisfaction with his team. He had a serious nature about him, and for years to come he swore that the team knew that they were going to arrest Allen, but let him fly back to Des Moines knowing he'd have to fly right back to Sioux Falls upon hearing of Allen's arrest. There was a debate among the agents as to whether Stump was joking or truly thought they had set him up based on his fear of flying.

From 9 to 9:15 PM, the investigators changed course and questioned Allen about his acquaintances, drinking habits, and job duties. Allen was unrattled, but so were the detectives. They continued to apply pressure, release, and apply more pressure through carefully devised questioning. They asked about his brothers, David, age twenty-four, and James, age twenty-one, and whether any of them had done any hunting in the last two weeks.

"Shot a tomcat outside the house," he said between drags on yet another cigarette. Then he quickly added that he also did some hunting on property just down the road from his employer's farm.

Johnson continued recording a note about each break they took and even that at one point Allen smoked cigarettes. The investigators' adrenaline kicked in, determined rather than deterred by Allen's obvious lies. All of them were diligent about not making a mistake that could hurt the case. They followed every procedure, including giving Allen a comfortable chair, knowing that court cases were lost on details such as a defendant being forced to sit in a hard chair under a hot light during an interview. It was 10:30 PM, and they had yet to garner the vital information they needed from Allen. The investigators started pressuring the laid-back suspect as a means to let him know they were on to him. They peppered Allen with reminders of evidence that linked him to the murders.

"You are employed at the farm where the female witness was taken."

"You were identified by her."

"Your prison number was eight-one-two, which matches what you told the girl."

Allen didn't crack, but he was agitated.

A different team conducted the next interview with Allen. Agents Pontius and Steinbeck, who had been itching to get a look at the infamous "Boss," along with Assistant Iowa Attorney

General Ira (Ike) Skinner, entered the interview room. Skinner had been quickly flown to Sioux Falls from Des Moines to help ensure all the legal issues were addressed correctly. Allen was told that his brothers, James and David, were also suspected of being involved in the Gitchie Manitou shootings. Those two brothers were in the process of being interviewed, and Allen was told he should be concerned about what they might be saying about his involvement in the murders. Steinbeck moved his chair closer to Allen when they sat down and straightened himself so that he was purposely looking down slightly on the suspect. In a commanding voice, he played his ace. "We have a living witness who identified you, Allen."

Steinbeck's bold statement sucked the last of the pretense from the room. Upon hearing this, Allen radically changed his story, but the explanation that followed cemented their belief that Allen never missed a chance to spin a tale in which he emerged the hero.

He slowly nodded his head and looked up from his lap with faltering confidence before launching into his newest yarn. "Me and my brothers had decided to do a little fishin' that night. I've been out there, and it's some pretty good catfishin'. We was down along the river just mindin' our own business when all of a sudden someone shoots at us!" Allen covered his head with his hands for effect. "I ducked down, and they yelled, 'Come out, or we'll shoot again!' I was goin' deeper into the woods tryin' get away when the bigger one came to where we was a hidin', and we grabbed him! You know, it was three to one. We overpowered him and got his shotgun. He did shoot once while we were tuggin' it away." Allen, with his high cheekbones, slender face, and animated eyes, gestured wildly with his hands as his story became more exaggerated. "We used anything we could, sticks or clubs. We had a big old stick, and I think if I went out there and looked I could find that old stick," he offered with a voice that attempted to convey sincerity. The detectives listened without interruption. The elaborate lie was a trap in which Allen would soon ensnare himself. "I rapped him across the neck and head, and he doubled up. My brother James got a hold of the shotgun. I said, 'Let's get the hell out of here,' and James said, 'Let them sons a bitches shoot now. We got a gun now.' I took off a crawlin' through the weeds as fast as I could go! Those guys were shootin' into the weeds thinkin' they was going to kill us. So we did jump and run just like deer huntin'—scare 'em, they jump and run. When I was runnin' I ran into a small person in the dark. I didn't know if it was a boy or girl. I was scared. I hit the person! It was a girl. I'm right-handed, and she was knocked out. She came to, and said, 'Who are you?' I said, 'Don't holler or yell, or I'll hit you again!' There was more shootin'. I seen lights comin' up by my pickup. It was my brothers who shot it out with them guys down by the river. They said, 'Let's get the hell out of here before cops come. We'll meet up by your north place.' I put the little one—the girl—in my pickup and drove off. When we seen those guys' pictures in the newspaper, we knew it was the guys who shot at us."

Allen rambled on, claiming that if they accidentally killed someone that it was done in self-defense. He smiled at his own ingenuity. Steinbeck remained stoic. He had the patience to listen to a crock of lies and then unwind the story to get to the truth. Besides, it was clear that Allen was not a profound thinker.

There was another break and Steinbeck agreed to remain in the room with Allen. Steinbeck offered more donuts and coffee, which Allen accepted. Now alone with Allen, Steinbeck used the opportunity to build some more rapport with the suspect.

Experience and training in conducting interviews taught him the importance of remaining calm and approachable despite the emotions churning in his stomach.

"We both have the same first name and even spell it the same way," Steinbeck noted, threading a small connection between them. By now, Steinbeck had the impression that Allen thought he was suave enough to pull the wool over anyone's eyes without detection.

Steinbeck asked a few casual questions about Allen's family and then slyly made his move. "Allen," he said quietly, as though advising a friend, "nobody is buying your story about those boys shooting it out with you." He paused and noted Allen's reaction, which was unblinking silence. "Come on, you should know better than to tell a story like that," Steinbeck said, continuing with the right amount of pressure while managing to convey that Allen could trust him. "We have the girl as a witness, and we'll be talking to your brothers, who no doubt will have a different story. The first one to tell the truth is better off. I think you should consider telling the truth."

Allen's brow creased. He met Steinbeck's eyes but sat deep in thought before replying with conviction, "Get 'em all back in here, and I'll tell you what I know." This time, a stenographer joined the group to take copious notes of the interview, which she later transcribed and Allen signed. Though Allen's story was far-fetched, his admission of being out at Gitchie Manitou the evening of the murders was a huge step in getting to the truth.

CHAPTER 21

November 29–30, 1973
Sioux Falls, SD Police Department

ALLEN WOULD TELL his third version of what happened, but it would be a long night. The investigators first talked to one of his brothers. By 11 PM, a South Dakota detective and BCI agent located Allen's brother, David, at his apartment on East 12th Street to bring him in for questioning. He was wearing a brown jacket, blue jeans, and boots with a large, metal buckle on each side. At 1:30 AM David gave his first statement to Agents Pontius, Steinbeck, and Assistant Attorney General Skinner. When told that Allen had already provided the detectives with information, David was unshaken. As though in a standoff, he locked eyes with Steinbeck, and the room went silent except for the distant hum of late-night traffic passing outside the window. The interviewers faced David from across the table; their strategy was to see if the brothers' stories matched, or if they turned on each other. During the interview, David revealed that he had a young daughter and worked at Seivert Towing. He was visibly guarded yet gave no indication of feeling intimidated or fearful and began by saying that he and his brothers were at Gitchie when they heard someone walking.

"Allen turned around with the flashlight and shined it up, and this one big guy was standing there with a gun. I said to Allen, 'Let's get out of here.' Jim took off running to the pickup. The guy shot two shots in our direction. Jim ran toward the pickup. I ran too. Allen jumped in and started it up—there was one guy by the corner of that little wind break and he had a gun and he shot. I stepped out and shot. I shot over him. I know I didn't hit him. I shot over him. I can't say for sure but there were more shots and Allen said, 'We are not going to get out of here. They are going to shoot us.' I jumped out and ran over behind the van and squatted down. I seen the fire fly from this gun and I shot in the general direction but I could see more fire back up toward the cement—there was fire coming from there. I shot again. From there on I don't know what happened."

There was a long pause, and David indicated that he had nothing else to say.

"Tell us about the two shooters," Skinner directed.

David's response was a scowl to convey the deep disdain he held for these authority figures as well as frustration at being unable to gain control of the interview. The tension swelled. Skinner had not risen to such a respected position in the legal system by being one to back down. He repeated the instruction with an authority that gave David no choice but to respond.

David said there were at least two shooters who kept firing at them. After the shooting stopped, he and his brothers found three boys lying dead and dragged them into the weeds to hide them. Throughout David's story, it appeared that he took the acts he and his brothers committed and placed the actions on the boys they were suspected of killing. David drummed his fingers on the tabletop. His fingernails, caked with grime, were long past due to be trimmed. The constant *tap, tap, tap* irritated Pontius, but he maintained a professional demeanor.

"I knew if we went to the police we'd be charged with murder. I wish we would have just went and got the police."

"What kind of guns did these boys have?"

"Twelve-gauge."

"How many guns did they have?"

"Three."

"Each one had a gun?"

"Yes."

"What did you do with their guns?"

"Threw them in the slough." David's jaw muscles tightened.

He went on to say that after this, Sandra appeared from behind the shelter house.

"She acted like nothing happened. Really I was shaking and so were my brothers but she just acted like nothing happened." His eyes glanced back and forth between the detectives, apparently looking for a nod of agreement but receiving none.

After that Allen took the girl in his pickup while David and James dropped the van off in Sioux Falls and got David's car before meeting at the farm.

"Had you made arrangements before to meet out there?"

David couldn't remember and as a stalling tactic he immediately launched into a story about a time he was arrested and charged with a Dyer Act in the late 1960s. "I swear I didn't do that. This car was stolen in Luverne, Minnesota. My brother Allen took this car. I was on probation and living on a farm working when this all happened."

According to David, Allen told the police at the time that David stole the car. They sent David to Willow River, Minnesota, a detention center, before possibly sending him to prison. On his first day there, David got into a fight.

"This colored guy came up and said, 'You white guys are no better than us black guys.' I smacked him." This almost got David sent to prison, but his counselor arranged for him to stay in the detention center. The same man picked another fight with David. Then a riot started one night and somebody escaped.

Pontius interjected, "What does all this have to do—"

David continued without pause. "I will come to that. When I first got up there, I didn't want to work. I was so upset because my brother done this to me. That is why I got in a fight." David told about lying in bed when the same man hit him over the head with a pillow, so David got up and clobbered him. The fighting escalated to other people, and the man who hit David got a hold of a mallet and hit another guy over the head. The man wasn't dead, but two of the "colored guys" were taken to the pen. Then two other men came over and "thought they were going to beat up on me."

The investigators listened while David continued a rambling story that kept branching off in different directions.

"They brought this truck—and these two guys thought they were going to get me. They got me down under this bench. I kicked the one and knocked him down. He was a lot bigger than I was. I couldn't handle him. I rolled out the back of the truck going about forty miles an hour. A counselor came along, and he thought I was running away because I was in the middle of the road. I said I wanted to go to the pen. I said, 'I can't put up with these guys picking on me all the time.'" Another day, David was watching TV when one of the guys smacked him and told David he was going to kill him.

"That is who I thought that guy was out there [at Gitchie]. The big, tall, dark-haired guy. I thought that is who it was."

The agents hesitated and considered the preposterous effort David used to connect such a convoluted story to the murders, and then one of them asked, "This is when you were at the river, and you saw this guy shooting at you?"

"Yes. You can check this out. *Everybody* heard him say, 'I am going to get you,'" David said bitterly as if acting defensive would make the investigators believe him.

David claimed he wanted to go to the police but Allen said no.

"Is Allen the boss of you guys? Do you and Jim do what Allen tells you to do?"

"No. Jim was in jail already, and the reason we couldn't come forward because Jim was in jail and would lose his working privileges."

"Is that the reason you didn't want to tell?"

"Yes."

David continued to explain that Jim left to go back to jail. He denied discussing killing the girl with Allen and claimed to have just left and gone back home. Neither he nor his brothers were drunk or had taken any drugs. He recalled that before he went home he threw five guns, three from the dead boys, one of Jim's, and one of his own guns, into a slough. Then the detectives switched the questioning back to the events at the park.

"You say you only found three boys out there?" Steinbeck sensed that David was changing his tactic by giving only the briefest of answers in an attempt to regulate the interview. David paused for longer periods of time before replying. He was struggling to maintain self-control.

"Yes."

"Did you read the paper?"

"Yes."

"Did you hear there were four boys? Do you know where the fourth boy was?"

"No, I didn't."

"Where are the cement toilets from the shelter house?"

"Straight north."

"What do they look like?"

"Cement."

"Can you describe them?"

"I can't say for positive."

After discussing the toilets, the investigators switched to asking what happened after he left the park and also about what shotguns and ammunition each of the boys had. David said he threw the shell casings into the slough, a statement he later changed. The investigators sat back and listened to the lies that continued to slip from David's tongue. They silently watched as the realization washed over David that he hadn't convinced anyone of his story. He responded by turning obstinate.

"Do you have a nickname? Do your brothers call you any pet name?"

"No."

"Do they ever call you Hatchet Face?"

"No."

"Sneaky?"

"No."

"Did you ever make any statement to the young girl about being police officers?"

"No."

"Did any of your brothers make a statement like that to her?"

"I can't say for sure."

David said that he and his brothers never discussed what they'd tell the police if they got caught and again claimed he wanted to go to the police right away, but Jim said, "They will throw the book at us." David answered more questions about supposedly hunting for deer when Allen turned his flashlight on a man standing within a hundred feet of them who "never said a word."

"He didn't shoot until we started running."

"Did you see the shot?"

"No. I was running." He explained that he and his brothers ran to the pickup and got in when another boy in a parka started firing at them.

"Then what did you do?"

"I jumped out, and I shot, but I know I didn't hit him."

"Where was your gun?"

"In the front seat."

"Where did you—"

"I leaned out the window," David said, evidently forgetting he just stated he jumped out of the vehicle. He insisted he aimed high and knew he didn't hit the boy who ran and disappeared into the dark. At the end of the interview, it was obvious that David's story was fabricated. Yet, he had a knack for trying to lead the investigators while remaining vague. He was no rookie to the hot seat. The interview was over for the time being. Steinbeck closed his eyes for a brief minute during a phone conversation to follow up on one of David's claims. Then Steinbeck headed to the next room to interview Allen again, not fully refreshed but refocused enough to continue doing what needed to be done.

CHAPTER 22

**Flashback
Summer 1967
Sioux Falls, SD**

Extremely deviant behaviors are difficult to forget even for seasoned workers in the criminal justice field. Thus was the case when Jay Newberger, a probation officer working with juvenile offenders in Minnehaha County, first met a teenager who would forever stand out in his mind, following a career that spanned decades. It was an encounter that would eventually connect Jay with the notorious Gitchie Manitou murders several years down the road.

In the summer of 1967, a series of frantic phone calls came into the Sioux Falls police station reporting that two occupants in a late-model, tan car were driving down the street shooting at people. Although there were reports of gunfire in three separate locations, luckily no one was hit. The first shots were fired near Rice Street close to Morrell's meatpacking plant. The second and third shots were in the Norton and Froehlich housing areas northeast of the city limits. A deputy sheriff soon spotted a vehicle matching the description of the one reportedly involved in the shooting incident, but the occupants also saw the patrol car from several blocks away. With red lights flashing and the siren screeching, a high-speed chase ensued. During the chase, the deputy lost sight of the car that seemingly vanished a quarter mile ahead. The deputy began a systematic search surrounding the last place he saw the vehicle and soon noticed tire tracks leading into a freshly cut hayfield, and tracks going behind a large stack of hay bales.

The deputy drew his .38 and edged his way behind the wall of hay. He found the car and soon had its two occupants in handcuffs. He then spotted a box of .22 bullets on the floorboard of the vehicle, and a quick search uncovered the .22 rifle the shooters attempted to hide among the hay bales. In custody was David Fryer and one of his relatives, who both laughed and joked about the shootings as the deputy questioned them.

Jay was assigned as the P.O. for David's case, which made it his job to talk with David and his parents, observe the family dynamics, and report a recommendation to the judge as to whether David should remain in the custody of his parents or be placed in a state facility for juvenile offenders. David was temporarily released to his parents pending the outcome of the shooting charges. Jay called the Fryer home, but David's father said he was too busy to drive in and meet face-to-face.

"I assure you this is a serious court matter, and if you don't come into my office tomorrow and have David with you, I'll have the sheriff bring you both in to face charges of obstructing justice," he curtly explained.

"Okay. I'll be there at noon tomorrow," David's father replied and hung up.

The P.O. office closed for lunch at noon, but Jay made sure he was there nonetheless. Without a knock, the door to the P.O.'s office opened and in marched not only David and his father, but two other brothers, Allen and James, as well. The four Fryers stood in a semicircle in front of Jay's desk, with cold stares, trying to act intimidating.

Though taken off-guard, the P.O. remained composed. "Go ahead and take a seat," he said.

"There's only two chairs," David's father shot back in what sounded like a challenge.

"Well, let me step out and grab two more chairs," Jay responded. But as he walked to the door, David's father stepped in front of him, blocking the path. Now the two men were inches away from each other in an apparent stand-off, but the P.O. retained the upper hand, being no stranger to dealing with difficult families.

"You can stand then, if that's the way you want it," he said and returned to his chair. Jay began going over various procedures and possible recommendations that could happen in the wake of David's shooting incident. While he talked, all four Fryers continued standing and scowling in an obvious attempt to intimidate with their four-on-one advantage.

Finally David's father interrupted. "I'll tell *you* what. If you send my chore boy away, and I don't have him around to help with the work, you'll be sorry."

It was all Jay needed to hear. "Nothing productive is coming from this meeting. I want you all to leave this office immediately."

The Fryers turned and straggled out. The words *chore boy* would forever stick with Jay. It was a term David's father would come to use repeatedly for all of his sons in place of their names. The connotation was both emotionally cold and heartbreakingly sad.

Then Jay narrowed down his recommendation to the juvenile court judge based on all of the information, including the hastily concluded meeting. It was clear that David would not be getting the proper guidance if he stayed in the Fryer home. The most obvious option was a state program placement, one that might give the teenager a new direction in life along with appropriate discipline.

It wasn't an option Jay considered lightly. He was personally familiar with the benefits that can result from a quality state juvenile facility since he spent time in one himself as an offender. Raised in an orphanage for seven years, Jay was well on his way down the wrong path by age twelve. He began stealing, fighting, and heedlessly breaking the rules of society and the orphanage. The nuns in charge were no longer able to control his wayward behavior, and he was sent to Boys Town near Omaha, Nebraska, where he spent seven years. He learned to work, be part of a productive group, and sang with their choir. His life eventually turned around, and to the surprise of the South Dakota officials who had originally placed him there, he was elected mayor of Boys Town while a senior in high school.

Jay finalized his report in which he made the decision to recommend that David be placed at the state training school in Plankinton, South Dakota. It was not just a lock-up facility but a multi-phased institution that had a work program, education, group therapy sessions, and many extracurricular activities. Each time he sent a teenager to a juvenile facility, it was with an intense hope that they would experience the same rehabilitation he did. The judge agreed to place David there for a duration to be decided by the training school administration.

The sentence did not have the outcome for which Jay had hoped. David cut his teeth on petty crimes and quickly moved to more serious infractions. The threat from David's father was taken seriously and Jay kept a sharp eye out when going to and from work, but the threat never materialized.

Several years after David was sent away, Jay found himself the Director of Court Services, which encompassed several jobs including overseeing the newly built Juvenile Detention Center in Sioux Falls. In November 1973, police detectives and two BCI agents came to his office with an unusual request.

"Jay, we have a high-priority situation, and we need your help," the tall, sharp-dressed detective began. Another agent stood by, writing in a notebook. The detective explained about the Gitchie Manitou murders and how there was a survivor, Sandra Cheskey, who needed to be placed in immediate protection. "She is in our custody, and we need a safe place to house her until the killer or killers are apprehended. We would like you to keep her here since this is a locked juvenile facility."

Jay began contemplating possible outcomes of this request. "I have to tell you, I don't like it," he cautioned. "For starters, I'm responsible for the well-being of the other kids staying here as well as the safety of my staff." Jay was known for his ability to quickly size up a situation and make efficient decisions. He was a model of assertive communication before the term ever became a buzz word, and his direct, *let's-find-a-way-we-can-all-win* attitude generally resulted in others following his lead. "At night we only have a couple of workers on staff. Suppose the killers somehow find out this girl is here. This is a very dangerous idea. I think you guys should find an out-of-town hotel and place her there with twenty-four-hour police protection."

The agents listened but didn't think that was a feasible option.

Hesitantly, Jay agreed to the idea. "Then I'll need additional protection," he insisted. Jay was adamant about providing a secure environment. He would compromise if they would provide additional police to patrol the area at night. They agreed. In the end, both parties got what they wanted.

Jay rose to management positions due to his many leadership qualities, among them his precise skill for thoroughness. Throughout the conversation with the police lieutenant, Jay considered not only Sandra but also the killers on the loose. How desperate would these men be to get to her? There was recently an incident involving a girl held at the center. Her teenage boyfriend was so desperate to break her out that he stole an earth mover, intending to crash through the fence surrounding the detention center. He was stopped by police before acting out his plan, yet the close call was fresh in Jay's mind. He called a staff meeting and informed them of Sandra's special situation.

"No male staff should be involved with Sandra in any way, and only female staff caring for her should associate with her," Jay directed.

There was still the concern of increasing nighttime safety. It was agreed that the most experienced staffers should be scheduled for overnight. Jay's own history as a juvenile offender gave him uncommon insight into the mind of a criminal. With killers on the loose, he forced himself to imagine the unimaginable. Then he decided the best possible way to deal with any difficult situations that might arise. Immediately, he set his sights on the most experienced person he could think of: a childhood friend who had once been his cohort in crime but who, like Jay, found his footing and now held a master's degree in psychology and was in the process of obtaining a master's in counseling as well.

Although Jay's childhood friend was in great demand, he honored Jay's request. The deep bond between the two friends worked in Jay's favor. It was a friendship forged from a shared history of lawlessness and intensified by a lack of family ties. This combination, however unfortunate, forever bound them together in a sort of surrogate brotherhood with emotional ties that perhaps superseded that of biological family. To Jay's relief, this friend and a female P.O. agreed to work the 11 PM to 7 AM shift every night for as long as Sandra was there. Jay could now sleep easier.

Jay would not place Sandra in one of the small holding rooms. The center was built with a quaint "mom and pop" apartment that was designed with the intention of finding a married couple who could be consistent nighttime staff members. It was currently unoccupied, so Sandra was put there, and her windows were covered with paper to protect her privacy. Later that evening, Jay went to meet Sandra. When he walked into the room, he was struck by the shell-shocked wisp of a girl. After a few introductory statements, he noticed her terror-stricken eyes. When she spoke it was with short answers, barely a whisper. Her first night there was exhausting. Hysterical screams from Sandra's room brought the female staffer running. But even after comforting Sandra the best she could, the nightmares recurred.

Then another problem developed. Over the next few days, Sandra did not eat anything. She wouldn't take even a bite, and with each day her thin body grew more strained until it appeared she might simply crumble. Jay was ultimately responsible for her well-being, a task he took seriously, and his concern soared. It just so happened that the Iowa court authorities sent an important child psychiatrist to evaluate Sandra since she would be the key witness for the state once the killer or killers were in custody. He stopped the psychiatrist one day to check on Sandra's progress.

"Sandra is in serious traumatic shock," the psychiatrist explained. "She needs to get some normal connections to anchor her to the world. Right now she is emotionally fixated on the horrors of that night and the sexual assault."

Now aware of her needs, it was up to Jay to formulate a plan. Sandra had made an immediate connection with Sheriff Vinson, a man she revered as a father figure. He was patient and kind with Sandra; he took extra time to gauge her feelings.

Jay knew Vinson from past interactions.

He knew Vinson was compassionate, a professional who was the real deal, so he understood why Sandra opened up to him. In kidding, Jay told Vinson, "I don't really think you're a lawman. I think you're a social worker."

But now Sandra needed a friend, a mentor who could spend regular time with her on issues not related to this case.

And then opportunity presented itself. College psychology or social work majors were frequently assigned to complete practicum hours by working at the detention center. It just so happened that a senior social work major from Augustana College started an internship at the center. Janet was competent, approachable, and fun-spirited. Jay called her into his office.

"Janet, we have a critical situation with one of the kids here. Her name is Sandra, and I'd like you to see if you can bond with her, pull her out of her shell. Just talk with her about teenage things, you know, girl things like music, movies, or whatever you think she'd like to talk about."

Janet felt privileged to have been chosen for this mission and set out to Sandra's room to meet her. Cautious not to come on too strong, she only stayed with Sandra for about fifteen minutes, but over the next couple of days spent more and more time with her. Jay watched over the situation like a doting parent. One morning he casually walked past the room and heard laughter from both girls. A short time later, Janet came into his office.

"Chocolate cake!" She beamed. "Sandra loves chocolate cake!"

Within an hour, Sandra had chocolate cake in her room. After that she began to eat a little during meals and even came out of her room to the common lounge area to watch television. But there was no sweet ending. Every day Sandra continued being taken to help with matters related to the case. The cake was simply a brief reprieve from her demanding role in the murder investigation. She missed her family, who was placed in a safe house, but the threat to Sandra's well-being was too great to allow her to join them just yet.

Chapter 23

November 30, 1973
Sioux Falls, SD Police Department

AGENT JOHNSON FLIPPED off the switch, silencing the hum of fluorescent lights. Even though it was very early in the morning, he, Vinson, and another investigator were preparing to take Allen out to Gitchie Manitou, to retrace the route Allen took when he left the park with Sandra. By now, the park was largely abandoned for the winter. Using only flashlights, Allen led them among knotty timbers and spindly bushes as though he were a tour guide. When they returned to the station at 3:30 AM, Allen gave another far-fetched version of what happened the night of the murders.

Steinbeck and Johnson, who had been up for nearly twenty-four hours at this point, sat across the table from Allen Fryer in the Detectives Bureau of the police department. Allen claimed he was ready to admit what happened the night of the murders. Despite the seriousness of the situation, he retained a calm demeanor and once again seemed eager to chat with the investigators. He started by explaining that his brothers, David and James, arrived at the farm where he worked between 3 and 4 PM while Allen combined a load of corn with his employer.

"Did you finish your day's work or was it quitting time?"

"No, we worked until dark."

"Did they work with you?"

"They rode around with me in the truck."

"What were your plans then for after work?"

"It wasn't dark so we went hunting pheasants for a while—fifteen or twenty minutes before sunset." Even though a few minutes earlier he said they worked until dark. The brothers were known in the area for poaching game as well as other illegal hunting practices. He went on to tell about going back to his house to have a snack and then heading to the Buffalo Trading Post.

"Did you buy some beer at the Buffalo Trading Post?"

"No."

"Were you drinking?"

"No."

"How long were you at the Buffalo Trading Post?"

"About an hour."

"What did you do there?"

"Had a bottle of pop and put gas in the pickup, then we started punching out on the rifle they was giving away."

"A raffle type of thing?"

"Yes—twenty-five cents a punch."

"When you left the Trading Post, where'd you go?"

"Down to Lake Alvin," Allen said, referring to a nearby, popular lake where he claimed they went about 11 PM and stayed for only a few minutes.

"From the lake where did you go?"

"Gitchie Manitou."

"What did you do there?"

"Pulled in and drove down where I said I parked the pickup—west of where the van was sitting down there in the bottom." He went on to describe the exact location where they parked and said they looked down on a fire burning.

"Did you have your shotguns with you at this time?"

"No, we walked down by the river, and Dave said, 'Look at them guys there. I bet they have marijuana on them.' And he asked Jim if he wanted some, and Jim said, 'Yes, I'll try some of that.' Jim never tried that before. He doesn't smoke. Dave said, 'Let's go back and get the shotguns and go in there and take their marijuana away from them.' They were really high on it."

"How were they acting?"

"Running around, hollering, and yelling." Allen went on to make wild claims about the teenagers' behavior, saying they seemed drunk, in an obvious attempt to justify his own actions at Gitchie. He was unaware that the investigators knew none of the kids had alcohol that night.

"Then did you go back and get your guns?"

"Yes, Dave said, 'Go back and get the shotguns and go in there and take their marijuana away from them.' So we went back and got the shotguns."

"Can you describe the shotgun that you had? What kind did you have?"

"Pump twelve-gauge." He went on to tell that he had 4-shot Federal brand shells while James also had a twelve-gauge pump with .00 buckshot while David had a twenty-gauge with yellow Super X 6-shot.

"We went back there, and we were just gonna scare them, and that's when it all started."

"Did they see you coming through the woods?"

"They heard us. One jumped Jim, and one fell over the top of him." He added that Jim was on the east side of the riverbank.

"Were you on a ledge looking down on the kids?"

"Yes, and I only seen two kids until later on, then there was three, then there was four. I never did see the one. The one that Jim run down. I never did see him."

"Did you know which one Stewart was?"

"He was the one that was hollering."

"Was he shot first?"

"I think so. He was hollering, 'I have been shot—I have been shot.' There was another shot."

"Do you know who was hit then?"

"No."

"Who fired those two shots?"

"Jim." Allen then admitted to ordering a boy and girl to come out from behind a tree but said the kids didn't say anything. Someone fired a round into the air as a warning, and after that he started switching his story around, first saying that three kids lay down on the ground before recalling that only two lay down. Dana was still behind the tree, and James went to chase one of the boys.

"David had the yellow shells or double-aught buck?" the agent asked.

Allen leaned forward and forcefully blotted out a cigarette in a plastic ashtray.

"Double-aught buck—blue." He started to spin a far-fetched story from which he never recovered. He even changed the type of shotgun shells David had.

"Where was Dave at this time?"

"He was standing there."

"You don't know whether he fired any shots or not?"

"No. The girl was standing in front of the tree and watching me all the time." Then the brothers started making the kids walk through the park.

"What, if anything, did you say to these kids as you were marching them up the road?"

"I didn't say anything. I said, 'Keep moving.'"

"What were you going to do with these kids?"

"I don't know." He said he didn't talk it over with his brothers on what to do with the kids, and that Sandra provided him with all of their ages, thirteen, fourteen, and fifteen. "All the time when we were walking, I carried my shotgun. I didn't do no shooting at all." He told about Jim checking Dana's identification but didn't know why his brother did that. Then Allen left with Sandra in the pickup.

"Was there any question in your mind about how many were boys and how many were girls?"

"Yes, I thought there were two or three girls."

"Because of long hair?"

"Yes. Because of their hair."

He told about leaving the park with Sandra and later meeting up with his brothers.

"What conversation was there at the farm?"

"A lot of different conversations. Them guys they wanted to hurry up and shoot her, and I said, 'No.' I said, 'I'll shoot her.' They said, 'Are you sure you can do it?' I told her when I took her there that I could get her out. I didn't want anything to do with any of them. After it started, it was too late."

"Who raped her?"

"Jim. I never knew anything about that until it was all over."

"How do you know that he raped her?"

"He got out of the pickup with his pants off."

"Completely off?"

"Pulled way down."

During the rape, Allen and David talked about what they were going to do next.

"I told David I thought we should go to the sheriff. That is when he blew up. He hit the ceiling. I was scared."

"What did he say?"

"Oh no, this is first-degree murder. They all have to go. Even that girl. She has to die. I never even answered him on it." Allen assured his brothers he would kill Sandra, but something made him change his mind. Allen waited for David and Jim to leave then went and filled up at the red gas tank and took Sandra home. He claimed to have thrown his shotgun in a stock dam and never once discussed with his brothers a story to tell the police in case they got caught.

"The next morning when Dave and Jim came out to your house, what did you talk about?"

"The first thing they wanted to know what I had done with the girl. I told them I took care of her. They said, 'Are you sure?' And I said, 'I am sure.' Dave said, 'If she is dead, they have no witnesses. They can't prove nothing.'"

"Did Jim and Dave ever tell you how they shot the boys out there?"

"They turned the van around and put the headlights on them. They said they just lined them up and mowed them down."

"Did they tell you what they did with them after they shot them?"

"Drug them into the weeds."

"Did they tell you anything about how they drug them?"

"By the feet."

"Were they proud of this shooting business?"

"No, both of them were scared. I was scared. I wanted to go to the sheriff. I told them we should go to the sheriff. That was the next morning when they come. If they would have been an hour or so later I would have been to the sheriff. I was just getting ready to leave. It was really bothering me."

"Why do you think they fired the first shot?"

"That I couldn't tell you. We discussed it when we went back to the pickup. Shoot up in the air and tell them to bring their pot on out. That is all that was said." They searched all the kids but only found that one had a bit of marijuana in a small film canister which James threw into the weeds."

"Can you describe what you were wearing that night?"

"Exact same thing I am tonight."

One of the detectives shook his head.

One investigator asked if either of his brothers had facial hair, to which Allen replied that Jim had a faint mustache but David was clean-shaven.

"How about yourself?"

"Like I am right now. I shave once a week. Saturday or Sunday night."

Finally Allen offered information about what happened to his gun, which he claimed to have thrown into a stock dam used for watering cattle. That morning, Pontius and Steinbeck brought Allen to where he claimed to have ditched his weapon.

"This is definitely the stock dam, and the gun has to be in there," Allen said with confidence. The investigators were leery of his story, but the water was searched by divers, and when no gun was recovered, they pressed Allen further until he finally came clean. "It's in my attic," he said, referring to the house where he lived near the abandoned farm where the rape occurred. Not being able to part with his precious shotgun, he placed it in a secret crawlspace.

The interview with Allen concluded at 5 AM. At 4:30 AM, Agent Smith obtained search warrants for the house and vehicle of Allen Fryer, and by 10 o'clock, several members of the investigative team, including the BCI lab crew that had arrived from Des Moines, were descending on his residence. At Allen's house, they had to remove a cover in the attic before reaching up into a crevice. When the investigator's hand met with the cold metal, the exhaustion from sleep deprivation vanished. He worked the gun out of its hiding place and raised it in the air as if it were the Holy Grail.

That same morning David's house was searched at 7 AM, and at 7:30 AM he gave a second statement to Johnson and Steinbeck. David was reluctant to proceed with the second interview, the main purpose of which was to locate the other shotguns.

Chapter 24

November 30, 1973
Sioux Falls, SD Police Department

"DO YOU WISH TO GO ahead and change your story as we discussed?" Johnson asked David.

There was a lengthy pause before David replied, "It would be better." The agents worried he was ready to clam up and withhold further information that could yield the most vital physical evidence, the shotguns.

David claimed he and his brothers went to Gitchie to hunt deer. He had a twenty-gauge with "either four or six shot. I can't say for sure." Jim and Allen both had twelve-gauges with either four or .00 buckshot. Allen fired off the first two shots, hitting Stewart and Roger. After three kids ran off and hid, Allen called for them to come out and then shot one of the boys. When they got the three kids rounded up and to the pickup, Allen ordered David to go shoot the two who were already wounded, but David said he did not shoot anyone at that point. Guardedly, he punctuated his statement with disclaimers such as "to the best of my recollection" and "to the best of my knowledge," possibly giving himself room to change his story in the future.

"Did Al and the girl take off about that time?"

"No. About an hour later."

"During this hour what did you do?"

"I ain't sure it was an hour. It seemed like ten hours," David said before explaining how all of the boys were brought up by the van. "Jim started the van. I got in the other side and he turned — backed up, turned it to the west which faced the boys, and he stepped out and he shot Dana Baade first and then Stewart Baade and I shot Stewart Baade in the back once. I think he was already dead because Jim was shooting double-aught buck and then he shot this Hadrath. He walked up and just kept shooting."

In later interviews with the brothers, the mystery of the blood trail and matted down grass was also cleared up. Stew, severely wounded, was marched at gunpoint by James. He was possibly in shock from losing blood. Feeling weak, he lay down and bled heavily in the grass but was soon forced back to his feet and taken to the spot where he was executed. After reaching the van, James put the headlights on bright to better see his targets; the boys stood squinting into the glaring light unaware of what was about to happen. When the shooting concluded, David and James dragged the lifeless bodies off the road and into the weeds. They literally had blood on their hands.

David said they put the shell casings in the van, drove the van to Sioux Falls, and got his car before heading to the farm.

"Did you discuss anything at that time?"

"My brothers were talking. I was so nervous."

"Did you overhear the conversation that the girl should be killed?"

"Not at that time."

"Earlier than this or later that you heard this conversation?"

"Later."

"Did your brother Jim rape the girl at the farm place?"

"No—to the best of my knowledge—no."

"Did you leave shortly after that?"

"Jim said he had to get back to jail."

"About what time was it?"

"I looked at my watch and it was three thirty or four o'clock or five. I can't say for sure but it was real late, and I said I am going back to town, and then Allen made the statement, 'I will hit her over the head with a club and choke her to death.' That is all I can remember." Then Allen took his gun out of the car. David left and threw the other guns, a twenty-gauge and twelve-gauge, both with pump actions, into the slough. He stood up and demonstrated how he threw the guns in using a sideways motion, almost like swinging a baseball bat.

"Can you think of anything else you would like to have in this statement?"

"I am too nervous."

Chapter 25

November 30, 1973
Sioux Falls, SD Police Department

AT 10:50 AM, SANDRA arrived at the police department, where she was shown a lineup of nine men, all with generally the same height, weight, and physical appearances. Johnson and Sandra's mother were in the room, but neither of them communicated with her. She identified both David and James and stated with absolute certainty that they were the ones who were at Gitchie. The police department recorded this process to potentially be used in court, which it was. In a later appeal, James claimed that he was shackled during the lineup and that he was the only one with a mustache. Both statements were untrue. At 12:45 PM, Allen, David, and their brother James, who was currently locked up in the county jail, appeared in municipal court, where fugitive warrants for all three were issued in regard to the Gitchie Manitou murders. The investigative team continued moving forward without sleep to gain more evidence against the Fryers.

* * *

Black smoke billowed skyward. Dry cattails and reeds crackled in a blazing fire. Steinbeck poured more gasoline onto another patch of cattails sticking out of the ice and threw a match to ignite a second roaring fire. Steinbeck was at Grass Lake with Detective Dennis Clauson and BCI investigator Dennis Smith, who was no relation to BCI agent J.D. Smith. West of Sioux Falls, the lake was actually a duck slough approximately the size of two and a half football fields. They were there earlier to have David Fryer show exactly where he threw the shotguns. The investigators were determined to find them. They first contacted the DNR to get permission to burn for better access to the ice-covered slough. Steinbeck only walked eight feet out onto the ice to burn off another cluster of dried weeds when there was a sudden sharp crack, and he found himself standing in water just above his knees. While the others howled with laughter, Steinbeck made his way back onto solid ice.

"You forgot your duck waders. Want me to drive back to town and get a life jacket for you?" Dennis Smith chuckled, breaking the intensity of the search with a well-placed jab. Agents in the field called it "gallows humor," comments that could sound callous or uncaring to anyone not facing the pressure of an emotionally grueling job such as these officers were facing.

"Great," Steinbeck said miserably, shaking beads of water from his boots. He was in the hyperalert, fuzzy state of mind that came from complete exhaustion; it had a way of making him overly aware of details. Their inverse ways of dealing with a high-pressure job complemented this partnership. Now the task for Steinbeck was especially unpleasant due to wet clothes. After the fires burned off the slough's dry vegetation, they began a visual search of the immediate area. Clauson saw something unusual sticking partially out of the ice. They started chipping a hole with a hammer, and anticipation mounted as the hole grew large enough to see that it was the gun's stock and magazine portion that was mired in the muddy bottom. David had removed the barrel of this Wessonfield twelve-gauge pump before flinging the gun into the slough.

The next day they went to the National Guard and borrowed a powerful metal detector with the capability of finding land mines. The sight of the metal detector made Steinbeck think back to his naval days as a radar operator on a landing ship tank, the USS *Jerome County*. The slough, though large, seemed manageable when compared to the ocean, which gave him a sense of confidence. The thrill of yesterday's discovery still pulsed beneath his skin. At first, the only sound was the biting winter wind rippling past their jackets, but then the metal detector started beeping repeatedly. After hours of tedious work, the investigators only found rusty beer cans, wire, tin foil, and a Pringles potato chip canister.

The quest to find the shotguns continued, and on day four scuba divers were brought in to assist. They hacked holes into the ice so the divers could access areas approximately six feet deep. They covered a large area, but in the end the divers literally came up empty-handed. The frigid waters of Grass Lake gave up one crucial piece of physical evidence that had the agents leaving the search victorious. Now they faced interviewing the most deranged of the brothers, and he would spin his own twisted tale of the Gitchie murders.

Chapter 26

November 30, 1973
Sioux Falls, SD Police Department

PHONES RANG IN THE background. A gaping yawn widened, and Johnson pored over a new stack of notes. Most of the agents had not slept since the night before the arrest of Allen Fryer. There was no more lighthearted banter or joking around. The work to tie up loose ends was extensive. That afternoon, another .00 buckshot shell casing was recovered from the park. There were search warrants to obtain and witnesses to interview who might have knowledge related to the night of the murders. Johnson lit another Kent cigarette. He bypassed a tray of donuts; he'd become numb to the normal sensations of hunger and weariness.

Johnson found something unsettling about James that went beyond having cold, unmoving eyes. It was James's unreserved confidence in situations that would have warranted nervousness in a typical man on the street. Instinctively Johnson's guard went up. Unlike with James's brothers, Johnson was unable to establish a connection, and James immediately began shifting the blame to his brothers. His first line of defense was to portray his brothers as criminals by saying Allen and David had been to Gitchie last summer and shot a hole in a beer keg at a teenage party, causing the kids to run and hide in the woods. On the night of the murders, it was David's idea to sneak up on the group of kids by the campfire. David returned saying, "They have marijuana. Let's get it from them." James assumed that Allen's gunshots killed one of the boys by the campfire.

"I took off running through the woods to the van. When Allen got back, he told me to take the boys behind the van and blow their heads off." James's cold eyes stared straight ahead, and he spoke with a steady, monotone voice. "I didn't do it. I tried to drive away, but the van wasn't running very well." He added that he saw the girl with Allen and that she was laughing and seemed to be having a good time. Allen was telling her he was a "Dick Tracy" detective and had made drug raids in California and even infiltrated the Hells Angels biker gang. "The girl said, 'I'll screw you all,' and went behind the truck and took her clothes off. Me and David both had sex with her. She never hollered or fought. It was completely voluntary on her part." He was responding with sinister calmness, and his lies spread like a fast-growing cancer. The next day, when James asked Allen and David what happened, they told him they shot and killed the girl.

Johnson remained expressionless as he took notes and listened to the spiel of lies. At 4 PM, an attorney was appointed for each of the brothers, and they all waived extradition to Iowa. On December 1st, Allen and David were moved to the Lyon County Jail in Rock Rapids, Iowa, but James remained in Sioux Falls due to the jail sentence he was currently serving. On December 4th, all three brothers were arraigned and charged with four counts of murder. Their bond was set at $400,000 apiece, which amounted to $100,000 for each slain boy.

CHAPTER 27

November 1973
Minnehaha County Jail, Sioux Falls, SD

AUTHORITIES HAD NOT GONE far to find James when they'd interviewed him. He was locked up in the Sioux Falls Minnehaha County Jail, where he was detained while waiting to be charged for transporting stolen goods. The jail had a work release program which allowed an inmate to sign out of jail to go to work and then return to lockup when finished. This program required approval by the jail administration. On the morning of the Gitchie Manitou murders, James signed out to go to his job as a tow truck driver at Seivert Towing. But instead of returning to jail, he had his brother David impersonate the owner and call the jail claiming that James was needed for an extra shift. The ploy worked, and James was free to go with his brothers, David and Allen, to poach some deer. However, the hunt for deer changed into a hunt for humans, with fifteen-year-old Mike Hadrath becoming one of the targets. James checked out of jail at 6:30 AM November 17th to go to work and did not return until 2:30 the next morning.

Standing six-foot-one-inch tall at age seventeen, Bill Hadrath, Mike's brother, was lean and athletic. His sport of choice was baseball, and he assisted his team in numerous victories. Bill's mother, Marilyn, proudly showed friends the newspaper clipping about Bill pitching a no-hitter in an important playoff game. The Hadraths represented a typical working-class family of the early 1970s. Marilyn was a stay-at-home mother who maintained their modest home on the east side of Sioux Falls. She doted over their oldest child, Bill, middle son, Mike, and daughter, Lynette. Her husband, Robert, put in long hours at Mielman's, a local packing plant, to support his close-knit family. Robert was a decorated WWII sergeant who earned the Bronze Star for action against the Japanese in New Guinea and the Philippines. His children would sit with wide-eyed fascination when he told them stories about the mysterious headhunters in the fierce jungles of New Guinea.

"Those headhunters practiced cannibalism against rival tribes and had skulls and shrunken heads hanging in their village. Our platoon stayed on their good side by giving them chocolate from our rations."

Marilyn and Robert encouraged and supported their children's exploration of various activities and expected diligence in school as well. They were not pleased when Bill began hanging around with kids Robert referred to as "riffraff." In typical teenage fashion, Bill discovered the hard way what a bad peer group would do to influence a life. He got into a few scrapes with the law, and when he sold some stolen items to a junkyard, the steely judge told him, "If you want to act like a big boy, you can see how this court deals with big boys." Bill was sentenced to ninety days in the Minnehaha County Jail. He continued going to high school but was driven back and forth daily to the county jail. He remained incarcerated at night, on weekends, and on holidays. He was required to maintain good grades and behavior while in class.

"This might be just what you need to get you headed in the right direction," Marilyn told her son just before he was led away by the court bailiff. It never crossed her mind to make excuses for his choices or appease him with encouraging words.

The county jail housed a variety of inmates, from those doing short stretches for low-level offenses to hard core criminals awaiting trial. There was a common area where all of them ate and could also play cards when not locked down in their assigned cells. Bill tried to keep to himself as much as possible, avoiding the older, hardened criminals. There was one inmate Bill found exceptionally peculiar. The man was quiet and heavyset with emotionless eyes. He was serving time for stolen goods, and his name was James Fryer. Occasionally Bill found himself sitting across from this off-putting man at meal times, and the man boldly inserted himself into a few card games on the weekends. His presence had an unsettling effect on Bill, who found the man socially awkward and physically repulsive.

On the morning of Monday, November 19th, a jailer went to Bill's cell about 7 AM and informed him he would not be going to school that day, which surprised and confused Bill. The jailer led him to a conference room, where he was met by his mom, dad, and the Minnehaha County Sheriff. Bill's stomach clenched and turned sick. His mom was crying. His dad's face was gray and deflated and had a leaden appearance that would never completely go away. Bill knew something was horribly wrong, and when his dad finally looked up at him, it was an act that took unbearable effort.

"Bill," his dad's voice cracked, "we have some terrible news. Mike and three of his friends were killed." He paused, and Bill froze while trying to make sense of the unexpected words. "The police are trying to find out who did this. We don't know what happened yet."

The words penetrated into his very core, and he hoped that this was all a bad dream. The family cried, hugged, cried some more, and then Robert told him more bad news. The room settled into sickening silence. Mike's body had to be identified at the Lyon County morgue in Iowa. The sheriff made arrangements for Bill to have a two-week hardship leave to be with his family during this time.

At the morgue, which was actually a room attached to a funeral home, the sheriff led them to a hallway. The building resounded with a nauseating gloom and a sweetly metallic smell, a combination of chemicals and the ever-present scent of funeral flowers. Bill expected to be shown the body through a window like he saw on television, but an attendant rolled Mike's body into the hallway. Robert put an arm around Marilyn's shoulders. When the attendant pulled the sheet back, Bill's mind went black. His whole being reeled. The pain of the sickening image pierced through their hearts. Mike's skin was a shocking blue-gray, and the physical trauma produced from the deadly shotguns was devastatingly evident.

Life cannot deal a more heart-wrenching situation than when a parent has to bury a child. Psychologists say the pain is indescribable. Almost immediately they began the task that every parent fears: funeral preparations for their son.

Mike's parents asked, "Where are his glasses?"

Mike was always seen wearing glasses, and when relatives and friends came to the funeral to pay their respects, the family wanted Mike to look like he did when he was alive. His parents didn't want their last image of Mike to be the one they saw at the morgue. Robert checked with a detective, who was unable to find any glasses with the physical evidence. The family assumed the gold-wire-rimmed glasses had been lost during the chaos of the crimes, so they went to an optometrist and obtained a similar pair with plain glass lenses.

When Bill returned to jail two weeks later, James Fryer already had been charged with the murders and put into isolation at the jail for his own protection. At night, alone in his cell, Bill imagined what he would do if he had the chance to be in the same room with James Fryer as he had previously. What Bill didn't know was that some of the other inmates had the same idea and would soon act on their plan.

CHAPTER 28

January 1974
Sioux Falls, SD Minnehaha County Jail

BILL HADRATH RETURNED to jail still getting through each day in an emotional haze. Alone, he ping-ponged through the stages of grief, going from disbelief to anger to unshakeable depression. A piece of his family's fabric was torn away by an act of violence from which none of them ever truly recovered. He forced his way through each day, going to school and returning to jail late in the afternoon unaware of the plans to get James that were rumbling through the jailhouse grapevine.

*** * ***

His timing had to be right. The inmate shuffled along, looking sideways and swishing the mop from side to side while steadily creeping down the tier toward the cell that housed James Fryer. Even among his criminal peers, the crimes committed by James were unacceptable and put him at the bottom of the jailhouse pecking order. In the world of lockup, crimes against kids mark the perpetrator for retaliation since many inmates trace their life's difficulties back to injustices they suffered as children. Those enforcing this code of criminal justice have the potential to earn status. The child rapist and murderer was unaware of the true motives of the inmate nearing his cell. The afternoon quiet amplified the squeaky wheels of the mop bucket being pulled down this wing of the old county jail. The sound was a hazily ominous warning of what was about to transpire. The enforcer was nearly in position to strike. Just a few more feet.

When he reached James's cell, the enforcer made a noise, and when James turned to look, a toxic fluid potent enough to blind came hurling through the cell door bars and struck James in the chest, stomach, and legs. An invisible cloud of bleach and ammonia engulfed the corridor, robbing the cell block of oxygen. Within seconds, two correctional officers hustled down the tier to squelch the incident, but they were overcome by the fumes burning their lungs. They coughed and called for backup in voices that came out as squeaky as the mop bucket. Non-affected jailers began opening doors and windows.

The enforcer, who was assigned a janitorial job within the jail, had mixed a powerful bucket of cleaners. He was transported to the hospital emergency room for treatment along with two correctional officers and James. The attack failed to blind James, and the enforcer was convicted of an assault charge. After this, James was moved to the state penitentiary, which contained an isolation area and was better suited to protect him from retaliation. But the jailhouse enforcer accomplished the message that one individual will act as judge, jury, and executioner as required by the convicts' code of vigilante justice.

For Bill, the attack hardly mattered. His family now represented the anguish suffered by the innocent survivors. For decades he rode the emotional waves of anger, depression, and guilt. He watched helplessly while his parents grew quiet and distant, never returning to the happy days that preceded Gitchie. Bill learned the lesson his mom so hoped he would. Through his own determination and the values instilled in him from birth through his parents, grandparents, teachers, and coaches, he rose above the grim cards life dealt him. He graduated from high school and went on to become a skilled carpenter. He raised his own family and continues to enjoy as much of life as he can, an opportunity that was wrenched from his brother on a foggy night in 1973. In spite of his generally optimistic outlook, Bill experiences regular regrets. "I was no longer Mike's big brother. He never got to have children, and I never got to be an uncle to his children." The ugly hand of death spread its tentacles through the Hadrath family even into the future generations that never were to be.

Chapter 29

February 12, 1974
Rock Rapids, Iowa Courthouse

David and his lawyer agreed that it was in David's best interest to plead guilty. While the lawyer was working to get his client the best sentence he could, David went ahead and signed papers without his attorney's approval. It seemed like yet another way for David to control a situation. Through David's interviews, several unsolved crimes that the Fryer brothers were involved in before Gitchie were cleared up. The Fryers had committed several burglaries and thefts. In fact, all three shotguns used in the Gitchie murders were stolen weapons. It was also determined beyond a doubt that the brothers had no connection to the girls who were murdered in Yuba County, California, despite the similarities. Allen's claims of being a narcotics agent whose work took him to the West Coast where he infiltrated biker gangs were purely imaginary.

On February 12, 1974, David pled guilty to the open charge of murder. The case was presided by Lyon County District Judge

Edward Kennedy. David admitted he killed Stewart Baade with a weapon. In Iowa, there are two degrees of guilt, first degree and second degree, so a hearing was held to hear evidence and determine the appropriate degree of guilt. Second-degree murder in Iowa is punishable by ten years to life, while first-degree carries a mandatory life sentence. David's lawyer said that the firing of the weapon happened so quickly that his client had no time to deliberate or premeditate. He reminded the court that David did not fire his weapon during the initial shooting on the ledge. Finally, the attorney accused the state of not being able to determine a motive for the murders.

"It's one of those tragic things that has happened. But there is no motive and the state has not established one and failure to establish one is to—I think to be considered by the court as evidence of second degree."

First-degree murder carries with it the conditions of being deliberate and premeditated.

David's lawyer argued for second-degree murder due to there being no evidence that his client was lying in wait for Stewart, which would result in first-degree murder. There was no evidence that the murders were part of a robbery even though this was speculated by the state. Even if he was guilty of impersonating an officer, this only carried with it a second-degree murder charge. Only with one of five specified felonies can a murder be considered in the first degree, and David did not meet the criteria for any of these.

The defense made an attempt to portray Sandra's testimony as being unreliable due to the fact that she was smoking marijuana. However, the prosecution quickly countered. All of the information Sandra provided from the start was truthful and accurate. Her admission of having taken only a few "hits" of marijuana was as credible as all of her testimony. This combined with an impeccable recall of her surroundings and how everything transpired that evening did not align with someone who was impaired.

Trumping all of this, however, was the consideration that first-degree murder includes the use of a weapon with opportunity to deliberate. The judge determined that a span of time passed when the teenagers heard noises in the woods before Roger was killed. After that, more time passed before the other boys were wounded and Sandra was taken from the park. Finally, the wounded boys were lined up on the dirt path in the headlights of the vehicle and executed. During that time, David had more than enough time to "appreciate the consequences of his acts and to deliberately and with premeditation kill Stewart Baade." The judge went on to say that he felt the Fryers knew Roger was dead and didn't want to leave any witnesses. The Fryers walked around the campsite after the initial gunfire and knew who was dead and who was wounded. The judge added that from that day forward it would always puzzle him why they left a living witness, but it was fortunate that they did.

The judge explained that he had to allow at least eight days before sentencing unless David expressly waived this waiting period. David waived this without hesitation.

"Now do you request that you be sentenced at this time?" the judge replied.

"Yes, I do, your honor."

"David Lyle Fryer, I hereby sentence you to imprisonment for the rest of your life in the Iowa State Penitentiary, at Fort Madison, Iowa, for the murder of Stewart Baade."

Sandra's and the boys' relatives were present, and they remained for the most part silent. David showed no emotion, and when asked if he'd like to make a comment, he simply replied, "No."

"David, as you now know, it only takes a few seconds to murder a boy and you pay for it the rest of your life," the judge said with finality.

When the judge announced the sentence of life without the possibility of parole, David was both stunned and angry. He was immediately transported to the state prison in Fort Madison, Iowa. Through his lawyer, he submitted a request to rescind his guilty plea before the sixty-day limit passed.

In an interview, David stated, "If all my appeals fail, I'll actually write the governor and ask for the death penalty. I won't live out my life in jail. Keeping me locked up for life can't turn around what happened. It can't bring those people back." He added that the shootings didn't seem real to him. "After that, I couldn't think straight. I thought more like an animal than myself."

The judge was not swayed and denied the appeal.

Chapter 30

**Winter 1974
Rock Rapids, Iowa**

THE TRIALS OF ALLEN and James would prove to be expensive and intense, and the media diligently provided the public with detailed updates. The prosecution stood poised to strike with Sandra as their star witness, incriminating physical evidence, and the confessions of the killers themselves. Of special interest, many wondered how the defense would counter all of this and what legal tricks or maneuvers they'd exploit.

When David's sentencing concluded, Allen underwent a psychiatric examination, and James fought extradition from South Dakota on the grounds that he was being held illegally. Allen was given psychiatric tests as well as a thorough medical test that would take at least three weeks. He expressed dissatisfaction at being placed in this hospital, complaining that he had no choice but to be there. Part of Allen's psychiatric evaluation centered on his lies about not taking part in any of the shooting and being the one to return the lone survivor to her home. He brought up a prior car accident from 1966 in which he suffered a skull fracture as well as childhood febrile illness, a series of fevers. These were possibly ploys to indicate mental unfitness. In a letter from the clinical director, Doctor Paul Loeffelholz wrote that Allen attempted to portray himself as being similar to outlaw John Dillinger. The doctor also wrote:

"He tended to fabricate stories and seemed to take some pleasure in talking about all of the possible criminal activities in which he had been involved in the past . . . This individual's apparent pleasure in talking about past criminal activity seemed to contribute to his feelings of self-importance. This is a bit unusual, but nevertheless does not manifest a serious mental disorder."

The doctor concluded that Allen had little capacity to have feelings for others and had little concern regarding his inability to empathize with others. Ultimately, he wrote, "This man is competent to participate in judicial proceedings. He understands the nature and quality of the charges placed against him and the consequences if found guilty."

Allen's trial began in February of 1974 at the Lyon County Courthouse. A substantial part of the prosecution's evidence was given by one witness, Sandra Cheskey. In addition, there were ten to fifteen witnesses whom the State's attorney said confirmed, expanded, and strengthened Sandra's testimony.

The defense attorney waived his opening statement, which put the ball in the court of assistant attorney general Joseph Beck, the prosecutor. He called Sandra as a witness, and the next several minutes consisted mainly of the lawyers and judge asking her to speak louder.

"The witness's mother is present in the courtroom, and she expressed some desire that her mother sit up here for moral support," Beck asked, and the request was granted. Though Lolo worked full time, she arranged to attend every court session with her daughter.

Sandra answered all of Beck's questions about what occurred at Gitchie Manitou the night of November 17, 1973, and then Allen's attorney questioned her. As would be expected, he attempted to make it appear that her statements were not consistent throughout the three interviews she gave. His questioning was designed to confuse her, and at times it worked. She was a young teenager with a limited vocabulary related to courtroom terminology: affidavit, de facto, habeas corpus, mitigating circumstances. The words were like a foreign language to her. At one point Sandra was asked if she consented to sexual intercourse, to which Sandra asked, "What does consented mean?"

The defense lawyer didn't let up. He walked toward the jury box then turned back toward Sandra like a shark circling its prey.

"Now, is what you said consistent with the statement that you gave on November 21st, 1973?"

Sandra paused, thinking back to which set of detectives she even talked to on November 21, and if that was the second or third interview. She seemed so small in the witness box, a child in an adult's world.

"Why don't you repeat the statement so she will know what you are talking about," the judge directed, and the defense attorney did.

"I don't know what I said [on that date]," Sandra replied. To the surprise of those in the courtroom, she maintained her composure.

"All right. Did you give the following statement on November 21, 1973: 'Those two guys came and shot a gun, and Mike grabbed me and pulled me behind a tree. There was a shot and Roger fell.' Now did you give that statement at that time?"

"Yes."

The questioning gripped her like a vise. The more questions she was asked, the more the vise turned, applying pressure tighter and tighter.

"Okay. So . . . is it true to say that you are uncertain if the time that you were pulled behind the tree was before or after the first shot was fired?"

"Well, it was while it was being shot."

"Okay. All right. Now, you are behind the tree. Mike has pulled you behind the tree. One shot has been fired. Now, what was the next thing you observed?"

"I observed . . . one to my right, which would have been Allen Fryer." Sandra demonstrated how Allen had his gun up to his shoulder.

"Did you step out from behind the tree to observe this?"

"No."

"How did you observe it then, from behind the tree?"

"I could see. They were far enough over that I could see them."

"Well, did you see around from the river side of the tree, or did you see around from the side of the tree that is farthest away? Where did you observe Allen, first of all? Did you observe him directly at the time that he shot Roger Essem?"

Sandra was in the gritty hot seat of cross-examination. The questions came rapid-fire. "Not directly, no." She saw Allen with the gun up to his shoulder following the shots.

"Were you able to see David at the time that Allen shot Roger Essem?"

The fast pace of the questioning continued. It was designed to create the idea that Allen did not kill anyone. As the trial progressed, the defense made a strong bid to sway the jury with conflicting ballistic accounts by claiming that Allen was not using number 4 buckshot, which is what killed Roger. The outcome would rest heavily on this one point. The defense needed to convince the jury that Allen's weapon did not fire the fatal shots.

"We expect the evidence to show—first they have referred to Roger Essem—that the size pellet from the shell that was fired from Allen Fryer's gun was not in Roger Essem. Therefore, we say that this conclusively shows he didn't kill Roger Essem." This statement stunned those familiar with the ballistic evidence, as it was contrary to the findings of the coroner and BCI lab expert. The defense continued.

". . . Allen Fryer and Sandra Cheskey, who is a little thirteen-year-old girl—and I'm not going to be rough on her—he [defense attorney] says that her testimony will show that they left Gitchie Manitou Park together, that at the time they left Gitchie Manitou Park the other three boys were walking around . . . So Allen Fryer wasn't even there when three of these victims were killed."

Upon hearing that, Sandra stiffened. Would her own statements that she gave in order to help bring justice for the boys instead be used to free one of the killers? It suddenly felt as though the weight of the trials was on her shoulders alone.

"That's the basis upon which I say I expect the evidence to show . . . that Allen Fryer didn't kill anybody. The evidence will show that the pellet size of the gun of the shot that was fired from Allen Fryer's gun was a number 4 shot. The only person who had any number 4 shot in him was Michael Hadrath, and Michael Hadrath was one of the people that was walking around under the surveillance of other people, under the guns of somebody but Allen Fryer, at the time Allen Fryer got out of there." He went on to say that when Allen took Sandra away, he could have "done away with her" but instead took her home. He was the good guy. And the burden of proof was on the State to show otherwise.

The statement made Sandra burn inside. She knew he was anything but a good guy yet had to keep her emotions in check, so she sat stoically, both anxious and frightened to give her testimony. Her mother had taught all of her children the importance of being truthful, and now the truth was all Sandra had to offer.

After that the defense questioned Sheriff Gene Gruhlke, who was the first officer to arrive at Gitchie Manitou that morning, about the drag marks that were found in the grass by the boys' bodies.

"You have no knowledge where they were dragged from?" the attorney asked.

"Yes, I do," the sheriff replied.

"Where were they dragged from?"

"It appeared they had been dragged from a few feet north of where they were reposing at the time I seen them. They had been dragged to the positions they were in at that time."

"You don't know how they got into that position, of your own knowledge?"

"Only by being dragged across the ground." Gruhlke did not allow the attorney to put words in his mouth.

". . . You're not testifying to this jury that you do know where these bodies came from to begin with, of your own knowledge? Of your own knowledge, you don't know?"

"I believe I do, sir."

"And what is it based upon?"

"Spots of blood and on glasses found at the beginning of the drag marks."

"But you don't know how they got to where the drag marks begin?"

"No, sir."

"And that's my question, Sheriff."

But it wasn't really a question that needed answering, as the sheriff didn't claim to see someone drag the bodies. The purpose of the questioning was to suggest that if no one saw someone drag the bodies, then it could have been anybody who did it, which was a ridiculous premise. Only one of the men involved in the murders had any reason to move the boys. The dragging of the bodies ultimately worked in the prosecution's favor since the event lined up with David's prior testimony.

During the trial, this continued to be the legal pattern. The attorneys dissected every event that occurred the night of the murders, and the defense tried to discredit Sandra while contending that Allen was not one of the murderers. The prosecution connected the dots. Mike was not the only boy who had number 4 buckshot in him as the defense tried to claim. Both the autopsy report and the BCI crime lab expert reported that Roger also suffered number 4 buckshot wounds. Allen even admitted that he used a gun loaded with number 4 buckshot. Sandra saw Allen with his gun up to his shoulder right after the shot that hit Roger. David Fryer, in a previous statement, said that Allen fired the first shots that killed Roger.

People were impressed with her tenacity. One day, Sandra had to testify for three straight hours. On the side, they began referring to her as "that tough little girl from Gitchie." And she remained tough as the trials progressed.

The courtroom was packed on the afternoon that the opposing attorneys made their closing arguments. The defense claimed that the type of shot Allen was using was found only in Mike Hadrath, and Allen left when Hadrath was still alive. Therefore, he did not kill anyone. The jury of seven men and five women went into deliberation at 5 PM, and their verdict came in at 10:10 PM on Monday, May 20, 1974. Allen was found guilty of four counts of first-degree murder. In Iowa, conviction of first-degree murder carries a mandatory sentence of life imprisonment.

Sentencing was August 13th. Allen was given a life sentence on each of four counts of first-degree murder to run concurrently. The prosecution and the tough little girl from Gitchie did their job.

James first agreed to extradition from the jail in Sioux Falls to Lyon County but later fought it, thinking that some legal maneuvering might put him back on the streets of South Dakota where he could slip away. When he served his time for attempted grand larceny, a warrant for a fugitive from justice was issued in order to keep James incarcerated. James, however, argued he was not a fugitive and therefore could not be extradited to Iowa. The ploy didn't work, and he was soon sent to Iowa, where he joined Allen in the Lyon County Jail. But the Fryer brothers had one more trick up their sleeve; one that sent panic rippling through the region.

Chapter 31

June 18, 1974
Lyon County, Iowa Jail

ALLEN WAITED IN THE Lyon County Jail for his sentencing date, and James's trial hadn't started. As though reenacting a page from an action movie, the two remaining Fryers managed a quick escape from the humble Lyon County Jail. It was June 18th, ideal weather for their outdoor adventure. Following the discovery of their escape, banter on the street mushroomed into alarm based on the fact that the Fryers worked as farm hands in the region. For the first time in their lives, farmers went to their barns armed with weapons. As if the brothers had not caused enough fear, anxiety now spread like wildfire.

A woman from rural Rock Rapids later recalled, "We didn't have locks on the doors of our house, so Dad gathered us all into one room to sleep. He wedged a chair under the door handle and sat up all night with his rifle fearing the Fryers would return to our farm where they often helped as hired hands."

Citizens immediately questioned how the escape was possible. The jail where Allen and James were incarcerated recently had new locks installed on the cell doors. Someone overlooked the fact that the new locks were not welded to finalize their security, but this oversight was not missed by Allen. Late one night, he removed a hook that attached his cell bed to the wall and used it like a wrench to work the nuts loose from the bolts on the new locks. He then took the jail cell key from the wall and went upstairs to free James. Loose on the dark streets, they crept about and eventually found a pickup with the keys in the ignition.

The brothers' empty jail cells were discovered the next morning. Vinson went straight to the phone and called the Sioux Falls police to get Sandra to safety. Phone calls to Sandra's house went unanswered, so Agents Johnson and Steinbeck were called to immediately race to the Cheskey farm where Sandra was living. It was probable that the first place the Fryers would go was to Sandra's location to kill the only living witness against them. Neither Lolo nor Sandra could be located until early evening. By that time it was too late to move the family to a safe house. The agents gathered everyone into the living room for a set of serious instructions. It was decided that the whole family would stay under one roof for the night with the armed investigators standing guard.

"If you hear any noise, any type of disturbance, stay upstairs until it gets quiet," Johnson said and glanced briefly at Steinbeck, who was going from window to window checking for anything suspicious. "Do not come downstairs for any reason. Wait until we call out our names and you hear us say, 'All clear.'"

After an uncomfortably subdued evening, everyone in Sandra's family went to sleep, or at least made an attempt. Johnson and Steinbeck went about their duty of securing the house for protection. The shades were pulled and curtains closed. By night, this created an impenetrable darkness, the kind that settles into areas that are beyond the glimmering grasp of city lights. The agents didn't sit back-to-back but rather in separate chairs facing opposite directions yet close enough to whisper in order to discuss any noises or movements they detected. Each had a sawed-off shotgun. They stationed themselves near the stairs so that if anyone did come down, they could quickly determine that it was a family member. Throughout the night, they took turns occasionally peering out the windows but never detected anything unusual.

In fact, the Fryers bypassed Sioux Falls and headed west, making it 520 miles away to Gillette, Wyoming. In yet another absurd twist of fate, they hit a pedestrian while speeding down the streets of Gillette. Luckily, the citizen wasn't badly injured, and witnesses were able to call in a description of the vehicle involved. Just outside of town, state troopers spotted the pickup, and a high-speed chase ensued. The troopers forced the vehicle off the road and without further incident put the Fryers in custody. In short order, Allen and James were back in the Lyon County Jail with its newly welded cell door locks. Vinson took responsibility for the incident, telling the press it fell under his duty to ensure the safety of the jail. His "no excuses" accountability was typical of the sheriff's approach to duty, and those familiar with his thorough ways understood that oversights were rare for someone as vigilant as Vinson.

***

Two grade-school boys stood with their Labrador retriever on the lawn of the Lyon County Jail looking curiously at the old brick structure. The barred side window held their attention, and the possibility of getting a glimpse of the occupant behind the bars was what brought them back here again. Their patience was rewarded and soon the shadowy face of Allen Fryer appeared. A disturbing smile crossed his face. He put his mouth up to the bars and began howling and barking repeatedly, much to the delight of the two boys.

"What are you telling our dog today?" one of the boys shouted.

"I'm tellin' him that he should go off huntin' and see if he can get a rabbit!" Allen replied. It became a continuing problem to keep the local kids from coming to the jail to get a look at or talk to the infamous killer from Gitchie Manitou. Allen enjoyed every opportunity to entertain the local youngsters by telling them that he could talk to dogs. A minute later, a patrol car turned the corner and stopped near the two boys.

"You kids get out of here, and stay away from this jail," Deputy Griesse scolded through the open window of his car. The boys waved to Allen and shuffled off in defeat. Eventually, a cover was placed over the jail window to keep Allen from exhibiting this strange behavior.

Chapter 32

December 3, 1974
Lyon County and Dickinson Courthouses, Iowa

On December 3, 1974, James appeared in open court and requested a change of venue on the grounds that he could not get a fair trial in Lyon County due to the notoriety of Allen's trial, which resulted in James's trial being held in Dickinson County. Right after this, the defense filed to suppress any evidence of a "supposed rape" in addition to all autopsy and crime scene photographs whose purpose they claimed was only to inflame and prejudice the jury.

Attorneys on both sides familiarized themselves with James's background by poring over a thick file of his past records. James was second from the youngest in a family of five girls and eight boys. He was born in Brown Valley, Minnesota, and at age four, the family moved to Roslyn, then to Groton, South Dakota. James's father was described as excessively harsh, critical, demanding, and overly restrictive. James felt unloved and unwanted by his father. When he was seven, he was bitten by a rabid cat and received rabies shots for twenty-two consecutive days. Since then he suffered severe headaches. He was baptized but never confirmed and complained that his father did not let the children attend church while living at home. In school, he struggled academically and was placed into special needs classrooms. He began getting in trouble and was suspended from school for fighting. He began stealing regularly and had even stolen a car by the time he was ten. In his teens he continued shoplifting and stealing cars to the point that his father committed him to the state training school in Plankinton. While on parole, he heisted a car from the school parking lot and crashed it.

A state psychiatrist determined that James had a full-scale IQ of 85, scoring low in both the verbal and performance areas of the test. This is considered low average compared to an average IQ of 100. When asked who discovered America, James replied, "The pioneers." He told the psychiatrist that he felt compelled to steal and added that "my dad is always crabby, growly, and critical of everything I do. My dad never loved or appreciated me. I can't go anywhere or join any activities." James requested to stay in lock-up or be sent to a foster family rather than going back home.

The psychiatrist added his own notes, which summarized:

"James Fryer has a fluctuating emotional attitude because of poorly controlled hostility, aggression, guilt, and anxiety. He appears to be immature, has feelings of inadequacy, and a defective self-image. Because of his father, James wants no part of normal rules or obedience. His intellectual thinking, however, is average and there are no signs of thinking disorders."

James was charged with four counts of murder, one for each of the boys. The judge explained that he could be found guilty or not guilty of first- or second-degree murder, assault with intent to commit murder, manslaughter, and a host of other charges that ended with simple assault. In order for a charge of first-degree murder to stick, the state had to prove several conditions existed, including that James shot with "malice aforethought and willingly, deliberately, and premeditatedly, and with a specific intent on the part of the defendant to kill [each boy], or the aiding and abetting thereof by the defendant." Because of this, the intent of the defense was to show that James didn't cause any of the deaths. If successful, he would walk away free. Although it was determined that James was aware of right from wrong and what consequences could occur from his actions, the defense used his upbringing as a way to gain sympathy from the jurors during the Gitchie trials.

James showed up for court dressed like a country western star with his hair slicked to one side and wearing boots, a blazer, and dark sunglasses. He was often cocky and freely smirked. As the trials progressed, the defense attempted to point the finger at Allen and David and to confuse Sandra as to what she actually witnessed on the night of the murders. When the prosecution moved to enter two shotguns as evidence, the defense opposed this, and both sides moved to the judge's chamber to determine the outcome. Without these key pieces of physical evidence, the case could easily be lost. After a heated argument, the judge allowed the shotguns to be presented. Then came more photographic evidence. Jurors gasped, hung their heads, and dabbed at their eyes. Any sympathy the defense might have garnered from James's dysfunctional childhood quickly evaporated when the prosecution presented the graphic and gut-wrenching color photos of the autopsies.

Sandra's composure was stretched thin. She had attended hearings and trials for months. Christmas, a holiday she used to anticipate with joy, approached, but even this only gave her a short reprieve. To make matters worse, she was informed that after

Christmas, David was going to appeal his sentence of life in prison without parole, which was the sentence he received months earlier when he pled guilty. He claimed that testimony Sandra gave during his sentencing hearing was not divulged ahead of time as it should have been. She wondered how much more she would have to endure, but she kept that heavy burden to herself. Her mom was working full-time, attending every trial and appeal, and meeting with Sandra. All night long, she slept alongside Sandra so her frightened daughter would have someone to hold when the nightmares woke her. Sandra heard whispers that kids at school were making harassing comments to her brothers about her involvement in the murders, yet her siblings supported her every day, never letting on about their own suffering.

Sandra never asked for a break; in fact, she insisted that every action be taken against the Fryers. "I want to testify about the rape," she pleaded. Those working on the case had never known anyone her age with such voracity for justice.

However, none of them wanted to put her through the ugly accusations that would undoubtedly come with such a trial. Both sides argued well. The jury deliberated from 4:15 to 10:15 PM on December 19, 1974, and resumed on December 20 at 9:30 AM. At 3 PM they announced their decisions: James was guilty of manslaughter for Roger and murder in the first degree for Mike, Stewart, and Dana. James was never charged with the sexual assault. The district attorney determined this was unnecessary since James was already found guilty of a crime that carried a life without parole sentence. There was no reason to put Sandra through a demanding and demeaning rape trial. Several days later, justice prevailed again. A judge ruled that David's initial sentence of life without parole would stand.

Shortly after this, James filed an appeal claiming he was denied a speedy trial. This was in spite of the fact that James himself created the delays, first by agreeing to then fighting extradition to Iowa. After that he alleged that he had "no capacity to consider or decide," which made him unable to assist in the preparation of his defense, so he was sent to Oakdale Medical Security Facility for a psychiatric evaluation. In July, he escaped from jail, which resulted in another setback. The court responded that the delays were due to his defense tactics and escaping from jail. For months to come, Sandra continued to appear at numerous appeals which further delayed her return to school. The appeals all fell through for the Fryer brothers.

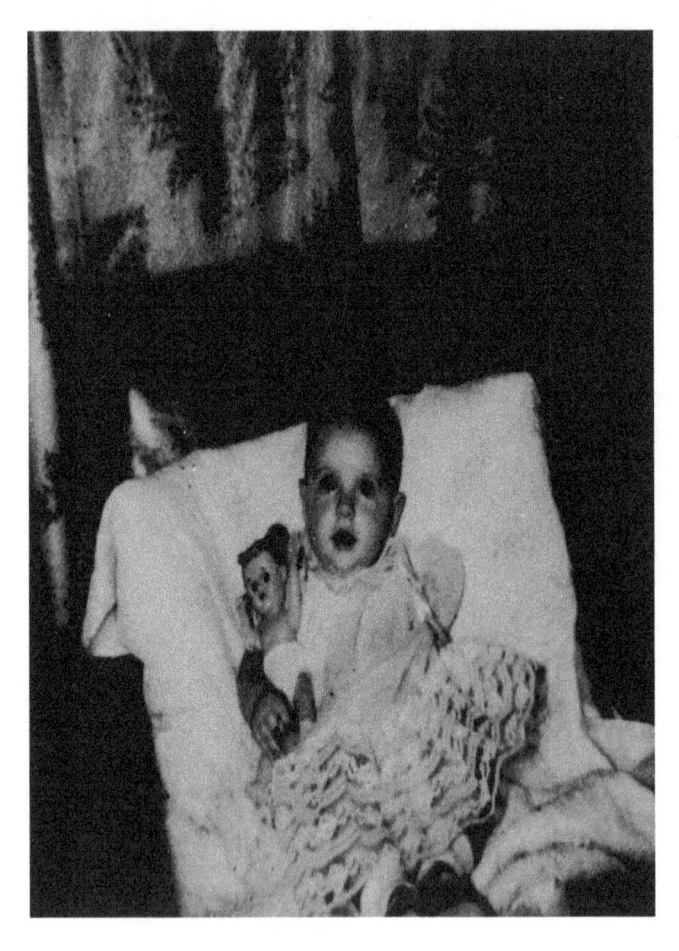

Sandra's birth in 1960 in the backseat of a '57 Chevy foreshadowed a life that would continue to be filled with unusual circumstances.

Despite working, going to school, and raising four children, Lolo supported her daughter, Sandra, throughout the aftermath of the Gitchie crimes.

Sandra's brothers have been an important part of her life. She is with Bill (left) and Jim (right).

Phil & Sandy Hamman // 171

A leisurely night at a state park turned deadly for the group of friends. (L to R: Roger, Mike, Stewart, and Dana.)

Sandra Cheskey was allowed to live with the condition that she give one of the killers her phone number.

Lyon County Sheriff, Craig Vinson, shouldered the enormous task of helping bring the killers to justice.

JD Smith prioritized leads coming in and assigned tasks to the team of investigators.

Jay Newberger was the director of the Juvenile Detention Center where Sandra was kept for protection as the search for the killers continued.

Phil & Sandy Hamman // 173

A few members of the Lyon County ambulance squad. Seated at the far right is Cheri and standing in the middle is LeRoy Henli.

BCI agent, Terry Johnson, headed the elite team of investigators.

Lynn Ford searched for the mysterious 800 number and acted as a decoy to draw the media away from Sandra.

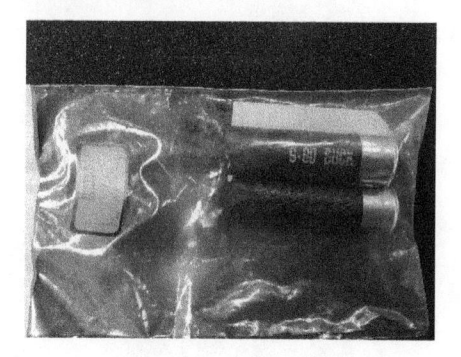

Spent shotgun shell casings found at Gitchie Manitou State Park.

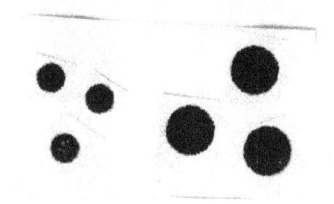

These silhouettes show the actual size of the BBs. On the left are #4 shot, and on the right, .00 buckshot.

Al Steinbeck created sketches of the abandoned farm and elicited the confession from one of the killers.

Bob Pontius was part of the team that went to the strange death house outside of George, Iowa. He was an integral part of questioning the killers.

This sketch accompanied Allen Fryer's interview in which he described throwing away the murder weapon.

The 12-gauge shotgun and magazine portion found in Grass Lake.

Deputy Sheriff Leroy Griesse and BCI agent Allen Steinbeck escort David Fryer from the courthouse.

The red gas tank outside Allen's house where he filled up on the night Sandra was kidnapped. She revisited the site over forty years later and found the tank still standing.

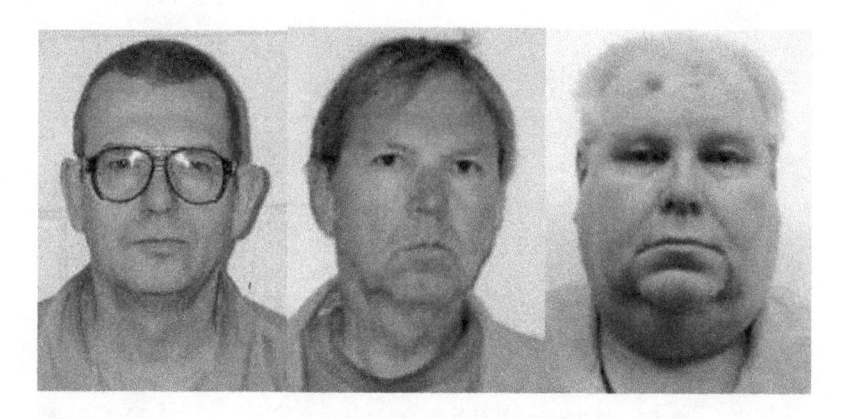

The three killers remain in Iowa prisons today, serving their life sentences. (L to R: Allen, David, James Fryer.)

CHAPTER 33

Harrisburg School, SD

SANDRA APPROACHED THE CAFETERIA, paused, took a deep breath, and whispered to herself, "It will be okay. It will be okay."

She stepped into the crowded lunchroom and inched toward the serving line. All around, the clamor of laughter, chatter, and the clunk of plastic trays intensified as more students filled in the empty spaces around the lunchroom tables. There was an electrifying hum resonating from topics regarded with teenage urgency: the football team's win, a new song topping the charts, and who was dating whom. It was the juvenile version of a coffee klatch, the time of day when kids could set aside their scholastic worries in exchange for thirty minutes of socializing with friends, and the mood was festive.

Suddenly, somewhere in the crowded room a few whispers sprouted, and the abounding laughter faded; their eyes shifted to Sandra. At the end of the serving line was that pretty girl who was rumor-mill fodder for over a year now. Hoping no one would notice her, she tried to blend in and waited until everyone else was seated and involved in lively conversation. She finally could go back to school full time after missing so much during the year and a half of jury selections, trials, and appeals. With the convictions behind her, she yearned to start piecing together her old life and trying to be a teenage girl, a life lost somewhere in society's judgment of the tragedy she endured. Cradling a tray of food and walking with downcast eyes, she passed between two tables to the gawks and murmurs of "There she is!" "She's the Gitchie Girl, isn't she?"

It was an era when the prevailing philosophy was that victims of rape were largely to blame for the crime. In addition, many students relied more on hearsay than news accounts and had latched onto false rumors including one that purported Sandra knew the murderers and was somehow responsible. Students could—and did—use every means to avoid Sandra. Yearning for nothing more than a friendly smile, she forced herself to hold her head just a bit higher and walked over to a few girls who'd been her friends before the murders. "Can I sit here?" she asked bravely, but the question seemed to vanish into thin air, and she stood there ignored and waiting for an invite. Finally Sandra looked around but didn't see any empty seats close by. Cautiously, she sat down by the girls who were seemingly ignoring her. In that moment, the conversation at the table shriveled. The girls rolled their eyes at each other and gave knowing smirks. Wordlessly, several of them picked up their trays and with glances of disgust moved to different tables, while the remaining teens shifted to the far end leaving Sandra surrounded by emptiness.

Although radiantly pretty on the outside, Sandra felt like damaged goods on the inside. It was as if she had watched herself progress in slow motion from a vibrant teenager to a dry, withered husk. She heard the comments. All around the school, gossip about the Gitchie Girl topped the list of teenage trash talk. Some longstanding rumors included, "I heard she was dating one of the killers." "My uncle said it was a drug deal that went bad." "She wasn't raped. She offered to have sex with *all* of them!" That particular comment produced a squall of giggles, and another girl added, "If she did get raped, it was her own fault. She shouldn't have been out there." The most hurtful comment was being told that mothers no longer wanted their daughters associating with the "Gitchie Girl."

Sandra didn't expect medals or accolades for what she did, but why didn't anyone appreciate all she sacrificed over the last eighteen months to bring justice for the boys? She knew the girls were under pressure from friends and family not to associate with her, but surely after a few painful weeks, their attitudes would change, and they'd once again see that she was the same person they knew before. She just had to stay strong awhile longer. In the days following the murders, the pain was nearly unbearable. With time, she learned to manage the heartbreak and fear. This was no different.

So, she ignored the whispers and began to choke down a few bites, all the while combating the hurt pushing its way up. She wouldn't cry. Not where they could see anyway. The tears were for night in her bedroom after her mom fell asleep next to her. With every hurt, whisper, and sneer of *"Gitchie Girl"* she added a new brick to her emotional wall. The wall grew bigger with every taunt. She wasn't just ostracized at school. It spread to public places or wherever she was recognized around the town. She drifted ghostlike through each day, clinging to the hope that the shunning would cease. But it didn't. The isolation became too much, and Sandra dropped out of school.

"Our Father, Who art in Heaven . . . Our Father, Who art in Heaven . . . Our Father, Who art in Heaven . . ." Sandra would recite The Lord's Prayer in its entirety up to fifty times in a row when she couldn't shake the horrible anxiety that came from the trauma that altered her life forever and enveloped her in darkness. Repeating this was the only thing that would give her peace. Night would come but not sleep. Insomnia became a nocturnal ritual. She would lie in bed and watch the clock's hands slowly rotate until the morning sunlight finally crept into her room. Then she would attempt to face another long and exhausting day. The boys and Gitchie were never absent from her mind. An emotional tattoo of that November night was eternally inked into her essence. Counseling wasn't readily available in the 1970s and was never offered to Sandra. So, she plodded through each day finding one way or another to cope the best she could. She held the hurt inside year after year and painted on a smile for those around her. It wasn't in her character to bother friends and family with her emotions. But Gitchie slowly ate away at her physically and mentally. It was a domino effect that started with anxiety and led to physical problems such as unexplainable skin lesions, severe weight loss, insomnia, and nausea.

Chapter 34

LIFE REGULARLY BRINGS "those" kinds of people to contend with, and thus was the situation that occurred a few years after the Fryer brothers were locked away in prison. One day Allen Steinbeck returned home after a day at work to find he had been subpoenaed in regard to a potential appeal to the Gitchie murders. After a few phone calls, he discovered the other agents who worked the case received subpoenas as well. It started with a group of instructors from a state university who went to the penitentiary to look for juicy appeals that could be used for teaching law students. A law professor from an Iowa university decided that it would be a unique learning experience for the students to see if they could get Allen Fryer freed on a legal technicality. The students researched the case, filed the paperwork, and prepared to go in front of a judge to argue for a mistrial on Allen's behalf.

On the date of the deposition, Steinbeck and the other BCI agents were there to defend all that was done during the arrest, questioning, and treatment of Allen. The agents were collectively frustrated. The state of Iowa and Lyon County spent an enormous amount of money to put the Fryer brothers behind bars, and a university wanted to spend more money to potentially release a criminal who was clearly guilty.

Smug about the possibility of overturning the sentence of a well-known trial, a professor and a semblance of students sat across from an unwavering Allen Steinbeck. It had the potential to put a glittering academic feather in the cap of anyone able to accomplish such a feat. The university professor alleged that Fryer was questioned for too long of a period of time, that the wooden chair he was provided was too hard, that he wasn't given enough to eat, and that the single overhead bulb was too dim. They fired an enormous list of questions at Steinbeck who, like the other agents, was able to refute with proof the baseless claims of each accusation. Fryer was given appropriate rest, food, drink, and bathroom breaks, and was allowed to smoke. He wasn't given a wooden chair, and the lighting overhead was not a single bulb but rather the standard rectangular fluorescent ceiling units used in all rooms of the police department. The group was provided with the psychiatrist's report that Fryer was indeed capable of understanding consequences of his choices and actions.

After hours of picking through the agents' every move throughout the investigation, the depositions went before a judge, who determined that there was nothing to constitute that Allen Fryer should receive a new trial. The investigative team had followed and documented every procedure precisely. He would remain in prison serving his original sentence. The process could have freed a cold-blooded killer all because a professor thought it had the makings of a good class project.

CHAPTER 35

THE TRAIL OF CRIMES left many unanswered questions. Why was Sandra out at Gitchie that night, and why was a thirteen-year-old girl dating seventeen-year-old Roger Essem? Sandra met Roger the summer before the murders at the concession stand of the Starlight Drive-In Movie Theater. Roger, who was friendly and outgoing, struck up a conversation. Sandra was physically mature and appeared to be older than she actually was. She did not go to school in Sioux Falls like Roger. She never brought up what grade she was in and only told him she went to school in Harrisburg. Roger asked if she wanted to go on a date, and the starry-eyed girl was elated. Roger saw Sandra hanging with her older brothers and some older friends from her neighborhood and based on a misinterpreted answer, believed she was in high school. In the short time they dated, she kept her age a guarded secret. Sandra's mother, Lolo, was going to school, working, and raising four children. Lolo was gone a lot, which gave Sandra more freedom than many kids that age. On the night of the Gitchie crimes, Lolo was working a night shift as usual, and in typical teenage style, Sandra left with her handsome older boyfriend and the other boys for a few hours of fun at the park.

Another lingering question is what was the motive for this heinous slaughter of innocent teenagers? Following an extensive investigation and months of grueling trials, a motive was never established. Those involved in the case and trials theorized that there was more than one factor that led to the night of terror. No matter what explanations were given, the obvious conclusion was that the Fryer brothers were dangerous sociopaths or psychopaths who lacked remorse. Psychologists have written at length about criminal sociopaths and their need to control. They derive strong gratification from dominating and manipulating their victims.

Leading from this was the idea that the incident stemmed from the Fryers' attempt to control the kids. The Fryers possessed shotguns and could do what they wished with this group. With their weapons, they had the ability to issue commands powered by the fear of injury or death, and this gave the Fryers the idea to march in and take what they wanted: the marijuana, the girl(s), and eventually the innocent lives.

The desire to sexually assault was on the perpetrators' agenda from the start. When the Fryers opened fire, neither Sandra nor Dana was targeted. Dana was young, had long '70s-style hair, and was wearing a jacket that concealed his body shape. Once the kids were gathered together at gunpoint, James Fryer personally checked Dana's ID under the pickup headlights. When it was determined that Dana was a male, he was kept at the park to be executed. This led to the conclusion that when the Fryers began shooting, they took out the males but didn't aim at Dana or Sandra, who they believed were both females due to their long hair.

Why then did only James Fryer and not the other brothers rape Sandra? Those close to this part of the investigation theorized that a sexual assault in a pickup was not Allen's or David's style, or perhaps those two were unable to perform in the presence of their brothers. Neither of them explained why they didn't participate in the rape.

Perhaps the most curious question is why Allen took Sandra home that night rather than killing her as he promised his brothers. Allen was quoted as saying, "I just thought she was too young, and she reminded me of my stepdaughters." This claim has been torn apart by those who see this as a convenient statement for Allen to make himself look compassionate. A more realistic explanation is that it was a self-serving act for Allen. Investigators quickly focused on Allen's "little black book." After he took her home and threatened to kill her if she talked, he asked for her phone number so that he could call her up sometime. Sandra spent a lot of time in the pickup with Allen, and he may have felt drawn to her. Did this twenty-nine-year-old deviant believe he could spend time in the future with this extremely attractive young girl? Certainly Allen showed he was immensely capable of developing wild fantasies on the spot. It is possible that he put her phone number in his little black book so he could call her later.

At the release of this book, all three Fryer brothers are still alive and serving their sentences in Iowa maximum security prisons. David Fryer came up for a commutation of sentence hearing in 2016, and he requested that the state prison board overturn the "without the possibility of parole" portion of his sentence, making him eligible for parole. David, however, faced two problematic obstacles at his hearing: Mike Hadrath's sister,

Lynette, and Sandra Cheskey, who are both determined to continue seeking justice for the fallen boys. Via a closed-circuit television monitor, Sandra told the prison administration why David's sentence should not be commuted. David, now with thinning hair and a creased face, sat with his forearms on the table, hands in front fidgeting slightly. Sandra wore a turquoise shirt and vest, her hair pulled hastily into a clasp after a sleepless night. In a steady voice filled with conviction, she read from a prepared statement:

"When David Fryer made the decision not only to deprive four teenage boys of their lives, he also changed the course of countless other lives forever. Roger Essem, Mike Hadrath, Stewart Baade, and Dana Baade were *brutally*"—Sandra turned to the television on the wall where David could be seen looking back at her—"murdered, cut down in the prime of their lives. These boys enjoyed movies, music, sports, being with family and friends, love and laughter. They had so much to live for." Sandra went on to list the joys in life the boys never got to experience and briefly recounted the events of November 17, 1973. "In so many ways, a part of me died that night along with the four boys. My life was and will continue to be altered forever with anxiety, sleepless nights filled with nightmares, problems with relationships, survivor's guilt, and post-traumatic stress. When David Fryer made the choice to participate in that horrific mass murder, he made the decision to live the rest of his life behind bars to pay for the price of his actions." Sandra faltered only briefly but remained dry-eyed. "And I still suffer to this day—noises in the night, memories, songs that don't go away. My friends died on the cold, hard ground that night. When I was leaving with Allen Fryer, Dana Baade had not been shot. Two of the other boys were wounded. My boyfriend was dead. David had the choice"—she turned again to the television—"to try to help those boys." Sandra explained that she doesn't know what happened after she left as she never wanted to know the details. "He needs to die in prison. I'm in prison."

Mike Hadrath's sister, Lynette, composed a letter that told how the crimes impacted her family. She told how Mike had just bought his first car that he was going to work on. After his death, the car sat in their backyard as if waiting to be fixed. He also had a new Springer Spaniel puppy he was in the process of training. The letter was read to the board members, and she listened by phone to the entire commutation hearing. A member of the parole board asked David why, in light of the terrible crimes he committed, they should make a positive recommendation for his sentence to be changed.

"Well, first, I would like you to know that I did not rape Sandra Cheskey. Another thing is that I pled guilty because I felt bad about what had happened." He then stopped, his statement apparently complete.

The parole board members paused as if waiting for David to add more to his brief and insignificant answer before restating the question and adding, "What have you done since then that would lead us to believe your sentence should be anything but life without parole?"

David looked slightly flustered. He wove and unwove his fingers a few times before answering. "Well, the way I seen the prison run, they go by your record in prison, which I think it should be, and I've had no reports, stayed out of all the trouble, and there's a lot of it in prison. And I've tried to help other people since I've been in prison. I talk to these young guys now and tell them they've gotta change their life . . . ."

When asked about his jobs in prison, David said that he worked in the kitchen at a different prison and worked in maintenance. He took graphic arts classes, was in AA, and was in a church group. If released, he would go to Davenport, Iowa, where a friend lived and had a heating and air business, though he admitted to the board that he had no training in this area.

At the end of the forty-minute hearing, all five board members explained why they voted not to recommend a change. David listened without comment or reaction, though a flicker of disappointment registered on his face.

During research for this book, the authors went to the Dickinson County Courthouse, where the murder trial for James Fryer was held. While searching through several evidence boxes, they came across Mike's gold-wire-rimmed glasses. According to the court documents about the glasses, they were found on the ground at the spot where the boys were executed, not where the bodies were found. At the time of the funeral, physical evidence was still being collected and logged, which explains why the detective could not provide the glasses for Mike's parents. Mike's sister, Lynette, is in the process of requesting that Mike's glasses be returned to her family. It is one final connection to the brother she lost so many years ago. She will likely have to wait as the glasses need to remain in evidence while the killers are still alive on the chance that they could be needed if the case is appealed.

What happened at Gitchie Manitou State Park was a real-life nightmare. Mass murders do occur but generally happen when a family member reaches a breaking point and goes after other family members, when a lone wolf attacks a crowd of strangers, or when something is gang or drug related. But a mass murder committed by strangers coming out of the dark is rare. What happened at Gitchie is the type of thing people fear when they are in a secluded area or are home alone at night. Roger, Stew, Mike, Dana, and Sandra were a group of friends who happened to be in the wrong place at the wrong time.

It is said that the devil comes to us disguised as evil people such as the Fryer brothers. He comes under the shroud of darkness just like what occurred at Gitchie Manitou on that dreadful November night. Yet, God's power prevails in the form of good people: the loving touch of an ambulance attendant, a committed investigative team that worked diligently for justice, and those who gave love and support to one branded as *"The Gitchie Girl."* It will always be the endless struggle between good and evil fought on the battlefield called earth.

Today, Gitchie Manitou is considered by many who believe in paranormal activity to be one of the most haunted places in the country. Prior to the 1973 murders, the area was a Native American burial ground. Some people who have walked through the area have reported the strange sensations of a presence. To others, Gitchie Manitou, now a preserve rather than a park, is simply a beautiful tract of land filled with powerful spirituality and scarred only by the memory of these senseless killings.

Adjacent to Gitchie Manitou is a pristine tract of land which is an ancient Native American village site. It is called Good Earth State Park at Blood Run and has been developed with winding trails and a majestic log visitor center. Inside, the walls are lined with floor to ceiling murals that portray tribes from the area. Gitchie Manitou Preserve will likely retain its name but eventually become part of Good Earth as the area continues to develop.

Gitchie Manitou continues to lure people with its lazy river, rolling tree-covered hills, and beautiful pink Sioux quartzite rock ledges. Others are enticed by its ominous reputation.

Chapter 36

Sandra pulls out a cardboard box, tattered and lopsided from being handled hundreds of times. She looks into the messy pile of mementos filled with memories of long ago. Teenage things. A headband from the hippie era. A photo of Roger, his hair shoulder length and coal black. He looks like a rock star. Other photos of friends with hopeful smiles. Slogan pins "Make love not war" and "Peace." Sandra sifts through the box reading old birthday cards and letters. She is once again a teenager reliving all that time stopped in 1973.

"I read once where teenagers who suffer trauma and sexual assault often remain emotionally stuck at that age. I suppose that is how I am in a way. I like to wear teenage-style clothes and do my hair like it was back then," she said.

But the tough little girl from Gitchie always finds ways to move forward with her life.

AS THE YEARS CREPT BY, Sandra tried to push the Gitchie memories deep into the recesses of her brain, someplace where the horrible images could be locked away. But the shadow of that night makes her wary to this day. After the boys died, a part of Sandra died, too.

"I was the youngest in the group, and the boys never let on to me that things were as bad as they were. They never cried or begged for their lives, and they stayed strong. Even Mike and Stew who were seriously wounded stayed so brave. They will always be my heroes," Sandra has shared repeatedly.

When Mike grabbed Sandra and pulled her to safety behind a tree, one can only imagine how frightening it must have been to be standing on the muzzle end of a twelve-gauge shotgun that is blasting away. People instinctively duck and run for cover, but fifteen-year-old Mike had the courage, the heroic quality, to save his new friend. After losing so much that night at the park, Sandra searched for ways to try to be near the boys, which began with her praying to dream about them. She played songs that reminded her of them, looked at their photos, and even contemplated suicide. She no longer had the boys whom she considered her heroes. Sandra lost her virginity to a violent rape, faced the scrutiny of the public, and endured eighteen months of intense murder trials in the spotlight of the media.

Through it all, Sandra transformed and would never be the innocent teenager who preceded the Gitchie crimes. Her self-esteem was scarred with shame and pockmarked with guilt, driven by the treatment from cold-hearted people. She battled back, and her resilience continues to inspire people. Sandra maintained a strong bond with her husband, Carroll, two stepsons, her mother, and her brothers. She found solace in caring for the many pet companions she's welcomed into her life, and she rescues animals.

She studied and got her GED. An amazing quality she possesses is her optimistic view of people.

She keeps a strong faith in God and uses prayer when drawn back to the terrible events of the past. If certain songs from the 1970s come on the radio, she may tumble into a depression but always uses the things she loves in life to move forward. When the first *Gitchie Girl* book was released forty-two years after the murders, Sandra slowly began to heal. It was almost as if the readers and those who come to the book presentations are her counselors, listening to her story over and over and allowing her to release the pent-up feelings. With *Gitchie Girl Uncovered* and more public presentations, Sandra's healing will continue.

Sandra had long wanted to go back to Gitchie Manitou with a small group of people, including at least one relative from the Essem, Hadrath, and Baade families. This occurred in the fall of 2017 when flowers and mementoes were placed in a beautiful location at the preserve in memory of Roger, Mike, Stew, and Dana. Prayers flowed and tears fell. Sandra no longer fears going back to Gitchie. She now has this special spot where she can pray and feel close to the boys.

Sandra still lives in the Sioux Falls area. Now she shares her story to inspire others to know that life can go on after tragic events. She thanks God for each day and enjoys life's simple pleasures, such as listening to music, watching a movie, going out for lunch, or walking with her husband. She adores her two stepsons and her grandchildren. She loves to have her nieces sleep over for a night of board games, shopping, and painting each other's nails. And, of course, she still loves chocolate cake.

A Special Note from Sandra Cheskey

FIRST, TO MY DEAR MOTHER, I regret that you were afflicted with dementia just before the book *Gitchie Girl* was released. You were unable to understand or take comfort in the way times changed for me. People who have read my story now give me love, hugs, and support. Mother, I am no longer ashamed of who I am. For so long, it fell almost entirely on you to be my rock. When I look in the mirror, I see you and how you raised me. I will carry on your loving and forgiving ways.

Thank you to all who took the time to read my story, which allowed me to release years of pent-up hurt and begin healing. To Carroll, my husband since 1986, I could not have asked for a more patient husband. Joshua, Jacob, and your families are always close to my heart. To my brothers, Jim, Bill, and Bob, you looked over me and helped me rebuild my life in more ways than you ever know. You are all gifts from God. To all my other immediate family, I am thankful you are in my life. To my aunts, Susan, Kathy, Regina, and Lois, I love you. A special thanks to Aunt

Susan for being a significant part of my life and Fran Henrich, who helped me trace my family tree and discover my relation to Laura Ingalls Wilder. I am thankful for my relatives who made it possible for me to have ceremonies for true healing and to honor me with my Native American name, Nahgi Okasa Wig, which means "Her Spirit Is Soaring."

Shannon Essem, you are a very special friend who always supports me. I will never forget the meaningful experience of meeting the Hadrath family and the five Baade cousins. To Joyce, who delivered me in the backseat of a car, I will always be Sandra Joyce Kaye Cheskey in your honor. Sheriff Craig Vinson and his wife, Betty, were the epitome of goodness. May you both rest in peace. The Vinson family is dear to me. I am grateful for the help and support from former Deputy Leroy Griesse and all of the law enforcement agents. I will always remember Linda, who drove Mom and me to every trial. I am grateful to Dr. Lornell Hansen for all you have done to help me. A special thanks to Talbots clothing for your generous gift. When I worked at Sweetman Construction, Marilyn, Russ, Donna, Rhonda, Betty, Mary Ellen, and my other co-workers became like a family. I will never forget all of you. Jim, Gary, and Julie mean the world to me. Karen, Pam, and Rhonda, you gave me a place to live when I didn't have one. There are many other friends who touched my heart.

For many years, I didn't think about how my mom must have suffered silently from being the mother of the "Gitchie Girl." She never said a word, but I know it had to have been difficult. My desire is that everyone who hears my story will use it to spread love and support to make our society a better place to live.

"Do not be overcome with evil, but overcome evil with good."

—*Romans 12:21*

OTHER CREDITS

THERE WERE MANY OTHERS involved in the Gitchie Manitou murder case, but when writing *Gitchie Girl Uncovered*, we chose to use only some of their names to reduce confusion. Listed below are the names of others who were involved in this extensive process. We express our apologies as we are certain to have missed some names due to the massive number of people involved.

Duane Barton, Crime Lab Technician
Joe Beck, Assistant Attorney General
Dennis Chapman, Chemist
Ron Forest, General Criminal Agent
Terry Hoil, General Criminal Agent
Tom Hopewell, Deputy Director, BCI
Chip Hughes, Vice Agent
Duane Lynch, Vice Agent
Andrew Newquist, Crime Lab Technician
Delbert Peterson, SD DCI agent
"Pat" Patterson, SD DCI agent
Tom Randolph, Crime Lab Technician
Charles "Chuck" Wood, polygraph examiner with the BCI

Others:

Ken Alberts, Lincoln County Sheriff

Richard Amos, Minnehaha Deputy Sheriff

John Anderson, South Dakota Highway Patrol Captain

Donna Barnes, shorthand reporter

Dennis Berreth, Deputy Sheriff of Minnehaha County

Bob Cose, diver

Dr. Jose Crespo, assisted with autopsies

Edward Cross, discovered the bodies in the park

LeRoy Downs, Sioux Falls Police Department

Dave Duncan, DNR Officer

Allen Fields, Sioux Falls Police Department

Monte Horn, Deputy Civil Defense Operator, Minnehaha County

Dr. Howard Gessford, medical examiner

James Green, Sioux Falls Police Department

Gregory Hansen, witness

Dr. Tom Henry, assisted with autopsies

Wayne Jepson, Iowa Highway Patrol

Elmer Kannengieter, Lyon County Engineer's Office

John Kottman, Minnehaha County Deputy

James McKelvey, Sioux Falls Police Department

John Mills, diver

Jim Pfannes, diver

Merle Remli, Sioux Falls Police Department

Gary Rhone, Sioux Falls Police Department

Dr. Richard Schultz, pathologist

Don Skadsen, Sioux Falls Police Department

Merlyn Sorensen, Sioux Falls Police Department

Wilbur (Red) Stangland, independent investigator

Judicial:

C.L. Anderson, attorney for David Fryer
L.P. Baker, Judicial magistrate for Lyon County
Joe Beck, assistant attorney general
James Becker, attorney for James Fryer
Don DeWaay, defense attorney
Francis Honrath, attorney for plaintiff
Robert Jones, attorney for Allen Fryer
Gene Paul Kean, State's Attorney
James Kelley, Judge
Jim Ladegaard, defense attorney
Robert Patterson, Judge
Hessel Roorda, attorney for defendant
Murray Underwood, Judge

All of the jurors who gave of their time to bring justice.

ABOUT THE AUTHORS

PHIL AND SANDY HAMMAN are the authors of the bestselling true crime memoir *Gitchie Girl: The Survivor's Inside Story*. The Hammans were born and raised in Sioux Falls, South Dakota, the hub of the Gitchie Manitou mass murders. Phil knew all of the victims of the Gitchie crimes personally. The Hammans' style has been to write *on-the-edge* true crime accounts. Previous works include *Rap Sheet*, which they co-authored, and Phil penned his memoirs *Under the Influence* and *disOrder*. The Hammans have been married since 1984 and live in Sioux City, Iowa, where they both have been long-time teachers. Phil and Sandy are blessed with two children and four grandchildren. The Hammans are popular speakers, addressing educational, church, and literary groups. For more information, contact the authors at philhammanauthor@gmail.com or via their Facebook page, "Phil Hamman and Sandy Hamman."

CPSIA information can be obtained
at www.ICGtesting.com
Printed in the USA
LVHW031035150921
697865LV00004B/320